# Making
# DOLL
# FURNITURE
## in Wood

by Dennis Simmons

Fox
Chapel Publishing Co. Inc.

1970 Broad Street • East Petersburg, PA 17520 • www.foxchapelpublishing.com

*Making Doll Furniture in Wood* is a brand-new work, first published in 2004 by Fox Chapel Publishing Company, Inc. The patterns contained herein are copyrighted by the author. Readers may make three copies of these patterns for personal use and may make any number of projects based on these patterns. The patterns themselves, however, are not to be duplicated for resale or distribution under any circumstances. Any such copying is a violation of copyright laws.

| | |
|---|---|
| Publisher | Alan Giagnocavo |
| Book Editor | Ayleen Stellhorn |
| Editorial Assistant | Gretchen Bacon |
| Desktop Specialist | Linda Eberly, Eberly Designs |
| Cover Design | Tim Mize |

ISBN 1–56523–200–3
Library of Congress Control Number: 2003107098

To order your copy of this book,
please send check or money order
for the cover price plus $3.50 shipping to:
Fox Chapel Publishing Company, Inc.
Book Orders
1970 Broad St.
East Petersburg, PA 17520

Or visit us on the web at **www.foxchapelpublishing.com**

Printed in China
10  9  8  7  6  5  4  3  2  1

Because woodworking inherently includes the risk of injury and damage, this book cannot guarantee that creating the projects in this book is safe for everyone. For this reason, this book is sold without warranties or guarantees of any kind, expressed or implied, and the publisher and author disclaim any liability for any injuries, losses or damages caused in any way by the content of this book or the reader's use of the tools needed to complete the projects presented here. The publisher and the author urge all woodworkers to thoroughly review each project and to understand the use of all tools involved before beginning any project.

# Acknowledgments

Producing a book requires the cooperative efforts of many people.

I want to thank my family for forgiving my neglect during the many months it took to produce this book.

I want to thank Jill Kennedy for the many hours spent converting my sketches into quality computer drawings for this book. She is a talented graphic artist, and I recommend her work to others who are in need of help. You can reach her directly at jkennedy@huntel.net.

I want to thank Dena Vittorio for her editorial assistance and project design review.

Thank you to Ayleen Stellhorn for the loan of her daughter's doll as furniture model.

Thanks to the editorial staff at Fox Chapel for their assistance and for giving me the opportunity to develop this book.

Thanks to the customers who purchase this book.

# Table of Contents

*Page 99*          *Page 120*          *Page 60*          *Page 140*

*Page 33*                    *Page 123*                    *Page 132*

# About the Author

Dennis Simmons has been creating wood projects for over 30 years. The rich beauty of various wood grains has drawn him to the art of woodworking. His inspiration for many pieces comes from living life in the rural Midwest. Dennis enjoys sharing his woodworking through classes with adults and kids alike. You may contact him to schedule a class in basic woodworking, doll furniture or intarsia by e-mail at **intarsiawood@hotmail.com.**

# Using This Book

I have enjoyed the challenge of designing and creating the furniture projects for this book. Furniture items have been designed to encompass a variety of cultures and time periods. The authentic furniture items are scaled to proportion for 18" dolls such as the American Girl dolls. These projects are designed to permit the craftsperson to construct heirloom quality furniture. All projects in this book could become treasured gifts for a daughter or granddaughter. I also envision these items proudly displaying a cherished doll handed down from a loved one.

These furniture projects are created with the craftsperson in mind. Each project is presented in a detailed step-by-step process from start to finish. The book includes simpler projects for the beginning woodworker, as well as more challenging projects for the advanced woodworker. All projects can be constructed using tools commonly found in home workshops.

I enjoyed creating this book and hope you enjoy making the projects.

Dennis Simmons
**intarsiawood@hotmail.com**

This picturesque bedroom suit provides a perfect play area. The drawers open and close, and the glass in the mirror is non-breakable. (Rocking chair plans on page 14; canopy bed plans on page 64; tall chest plans on page 90; short chest plans on page 99; mirror plans on page 132.)

The focal point of this simple dining room set is the stately grandfather clock in the corner. The front of the clock cabinet opens and a working time piece graces the top. (Dining chair plans on page 26; dining table plans on page 51; bookcase plans on page 120; grandfather clock plans on page 123.)

An Adirondack chair and table and a picnic table make a great outdoor set. Keep the planks small to provide a more scaled look. (Adirondack chair plans on page 33; Adirondack table plans on page 48; picnic table plans on page 56.)

Angled cuts created with a scroll saw give this bedroom suit a southwestern charm. Wood with a small grain pattern helps to give the furniture a realistic look. (Southwestern nightstand plans on page 60; southwestern bed plans on page 77; treasure chest plans on page 116.)

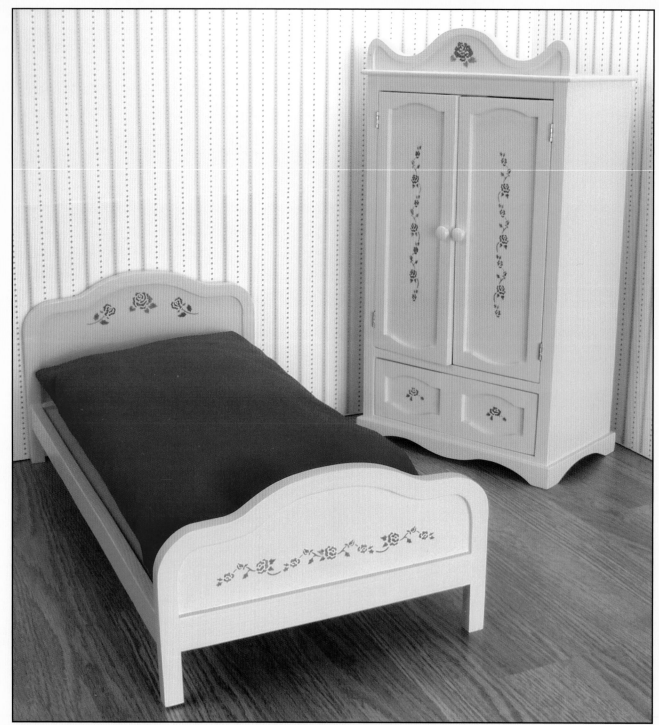

Any of the furniture in this book can be painted. Here yellow acrylic paint and stenciled roses adorn a classic bedroom set. The doors of the armoire open to reveal a hanging rod. (Classic bed plans on page 83; armoire plans on page 107.)

# Part One

# Getting Started

There are a number of points that a woodworker needs to keep in mind as he or she sets about making wooden furniture for dolls. This chapter will provide instruction and insight on the basics.

## Recommended tools

All of the projects in this book were made using common woodworking tools. You will need the following basic tools to make doll furniture. Certain projects in this book may require additional tools.

*Power tools*
Scroll saw
Band saw
Table saw
Miter saw
Router
Drill press with mortise attachment
Jointer
Thickness planer

*Hand tools*
Steel square, 3"–6"
Small-sized bar clamps
Steel scale, 6"
Calipers, 6"–8"
Mini bench vise (optional)

## Patterns and drawings

Drawings are provided for each individual furniture part needed to make the projects. Some drawings have side views or end views; others do not. Side or end views are provided only when the piece has a special feature that needs additional explanation. Drawings are not provided for simple rectangular parts. Measurement for these parts are included in the materials list. Drawings have been made full-size when possible. Some full-sized drawings have a section removed (indicated by a wavy line). This technique permits those drawings to fit on the printed page. Other drawings that could not fit on the printed page have been reduced to permit

Along with a sharpened pencil and measuring devices, you will need a depth gage (in my hand) a caliper (bottom right) and a combination square (bottom left).

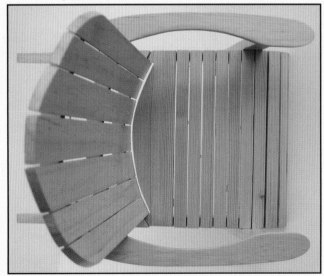

Notice how the narrow grain pattern in the wood on this Adirondack chair gives the chair an authentic look. Wood with a wider grain pattern would give the chair an odd appearance.

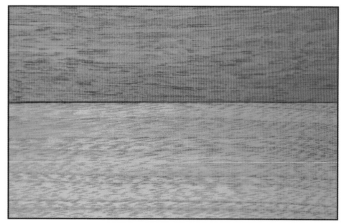

The difference between fine-grained wood in the darker board and coarse-grained wood in the lighter board is apparent in this photograph. Choose fine-grained wood for high quality doll furniture.

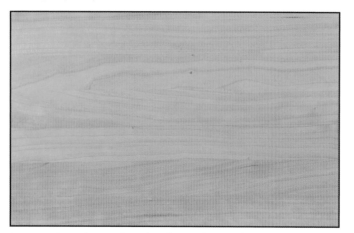

Narrow boards can be glued together to form a larger board to make doll furniture look more authentic.

Sawing a board through its thickness will result in two or more thinner boards. This technique is called re-sawing and is useful in creating the thinner boards needed for doll furniture construction.

Smoothing boards that have been re-sawn is a necessity and can be done with a thickness planer, as shown here, or with a jointer.

the entire part to be shown. These drawings can be enlarged with the aid of a photocopy machine to create the full-sized patterns. The percentage for enlargement appears on the drawing. A symbol is used near the drawing name on each drawing to indicate the recommended direction of the wood grain.

Some of the furniture pieces in this book have decorative, curved shapes that are difficult to dimension. This problem can easily be resolved. Full-sized paper patterns of any piece can be made using a photocopy machine. The photocopy paper pattern can then be attached to the wood piece using a temporary adhesive. Follow the lines on the paper pattern when cutting the decorative shape. Temporary mounting adhesives are available from arts and crafts stores and office supply stores.

## Wood selection

Fine-grained hardwood is recommended for the doll furniture pieces. Clear, straight-grained boards should be selected. Boards normally have variations in grain line width. The wider grain pattern sections normally found in boards are out of scale when making miniature furniture. When making doll furniture, strive to choose boards or sections of boards with the narrowest grain lines possible. The narrower the grain lines, the more authentic the finished furniture piece will look.

Clamps (shown above and at right) ensure that the project stays square and dries correctly.

## Authentic wood panels

Cabinet sides, tabletops and chair seats are examples of full-sized furniture pieces that are made from wide wood panels. Wide wood panels are made from several boards glued together to form a larger panel. Gluing boards together in full-sized furniture is a must because wide boards are not available. However, gluing boards together when making doll furniture is optional.

To make doll furniture look authentic, glue narrow boards together to form larger panels. Plywood can be used when making panels to simplify construction.

## Making thin wood

The doll furniture projects in this book require the use of wood ranging from ⅛" – ¾" thick. Thin wood can be purchased at specialty wood supply stores or by mail order. Check the yellow pages of your local phone book or do an Internet search to find suppliers.

Standard ¾" and 1½" thick boards can be cut into thinner boards using a technique called re-sawing. Re-sawing refers to cutting a board through the thickness into two or more thinner boards. Re-sawing is most often done using a band saw or a table saw. Narrower width boards, 1½" or less, can be re-sawn on a scroll saw. The thin boards cut by re-sawing will require the use of a thickness planer or jointer to remove saw blade marks and to ensure a consistent thickness.

## Recommended fasteners

For safety reasons avoid using metal fasteners. If the furniture piece becomes broken through play or by accident, a child could be injured on a sharp metal fastener.

In addition, screws and brad nails have a limited selection in miniature sizes, and their use in hardwood can easily cause the wood to split. I use these items judiciously in the projects that follow, and I would have limited their use even more if the final projects were intended for use by children.

Well-constructed glue joints are stronger than the wood itself and often need no additional fastener. Yellow wood glue was my glue of choice for all of the projects in this book. A small artist paintbrush may be used to apply glue to small parts. Excess wood glue should be promptly removed from areas where a finish will be applied. Glue will not permit stain or finish to penetrate, thus causing an unsightly final project.

## Recommended hardware

The materials list for each project includes the recommended size for the hardware items required to make that particular project. Miniature hinges and screws are available but are more difficult to find. All hardware items used in this book were purchased from mail order suppliers. Refer to the yellow pages of your local phone book or do an Internet search to find suppliers.

## Finishing

Wipe-on polyurethane finish was used on the varnished projects in this book. Danish oil or tung oil will also work well. Follow the manufacturer's directions for use of these products. If child safety is a great concern, use finishes formulated for use on food containers such

Making sure that all the pieces are square is an important step to ensuring that the piece is level and stands correctly.

as Toy & Salad Bowl Finish. Non-toxic acrylic paints were used on the painted projects in this book.

## Accuracy

Accurate measurements and precise cutting are required when making smaller projects like doll furniture. An inexpensive pair of calipers is helpful when measuring small pieces. Calipers can be used to measure outside dimensions, inside dimensions and depths.

## Safety

Safety is the responsibility of the craftsperson using the tools. This book is not intended to teach the proper or safe usage of any tools mentioned. It is the responsibility of the craftsperson to read and follow all safety

information provided with any tools used. Some photos in this book show power tools with safety guards removed to provide a clear view for photography. When working with power tools in your shop, use guards and manufacturer-recommended safety gear at all times.

Cutting small pieces of wood with power tools can be dangerous if not done properly. When possible cut rabbets, dados and miters before removing the small piece of furniture from the larger board.

# Wood joint primer

Several wood joints are used repeatedly throughout the projects in this book. Below is a quick look at these joints. If you are a beginning woodworker, refer to books on the subject of joints or take a class at a local wood-working store. It is imperative that you understand these joints and how to use the tools that create them before you begin the projects in this book.

## Butt joint

A butt joint is one of the easiest joints to make. The square end of one board is joined with a flat surface on the second board. The joint is held together with glue when making doll furniture.

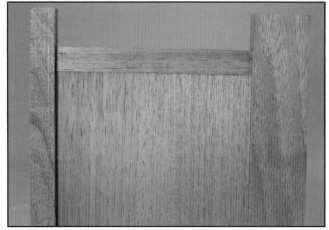

An easy joint, the butt joint is made by gluing the edge of one board to the flat surface of a second board.

## Edge joint

Use a jointer to smooth the edges of the boards to be joined by an edge joint.

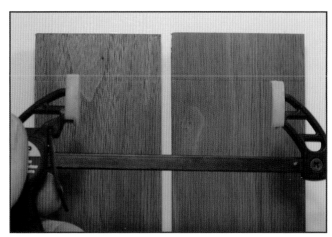

Use a jointer to smooth the edges of the boards to be joined by an edge joint.

When two or more boards are placed edge to edge and glued together to make a wider board, this is called an edge joint. The edges of the boards to be joined need to be straight and square with the face. The edges should be smoothed using a hand plane or power joint-er. Use glue and bar clamps or pipe clamps to hold the boards in alignment until the glue dries.

## Dado joint

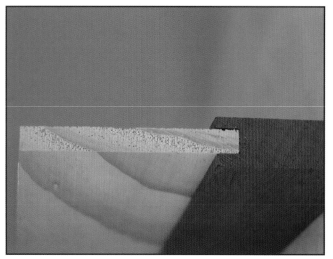

A dado joint allows two boards to be joined with a three-sided cut.

A table-mounted router or a table saw can be used to cut a dado, which is a three-sided cut.

A dado joint consists of a three-sided groove cut in the face of the first board and to a depth of one-fourth to one-half the thickness of the first board. The width of the groove is usually equal to the thickness of the second board. A dado groove can be cut using a table-mounted router or table saw.

## Rabbet joint

The L-shaped cut of a rabbet joint can be cut with a router or table saw.

A rabbet joint requires an L-shaped groove to be cut across the end or edge of the first board. The groove is usually cut into the first board to one-half to two-thirds of the first board's thickness. The groove width is equal to the thickness of the second board to be joined. A rabbet groove can be cut using a router or table saw.

## Miter joint

A miter joint joins two angled pieces of wood.

A miter joint joins two pieces of wood cut at complementary angles. Both boards to be joined have an angle cut on mating surfaces. The angle is usually one-half of the total angle of the finished joint. For example, a 90-degree corner would require miter cuts of 45 degrees. A flat miter joint is commonly seen in picture frames to hide end grain. An edge miter joint is used to hide end grain when making boxes. This joint is used in the treasure box project.

## Mortise-and-tenon joint

A mortise-and-tenon joint comprises a square or rectangular peg and a matching hole.

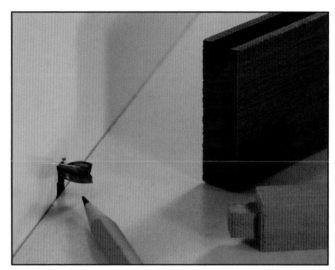

A table router can be used to cut the mortise, the recessed area, of a mortise-and-tenon joint.

This joint is a square or rectangular peg cut on the end of the first piece to be joined. A mating square or rectangular hole is cut into the face of the second piece to be joined. The mortise is cut using a mortise attach-ment on a drill press or a mortising machine. The tenon can be cut using a table router, band saw or scroll saw. This joint is used in the bed, chest and chair sections of this book.

## Mortise-and-tenon joint (continued)

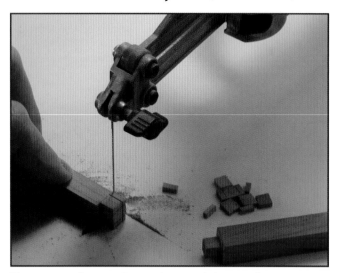

The tenon of a mortise-and-tenon joint can be cut on a scroll saw.

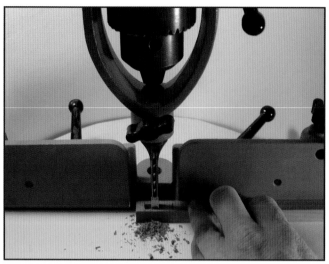

A mortise drill provides a specialized option for cutting mortises.

# Part Two

# Doll Chairs

Page 14

Page 26

Page 33

Page 39

**F**irst and foremost, a doll should have a chair. Whether the doll is an heirloom poised on a shelf for safekeeping or a treasured companion of a small child, a chair is a necessity. Chairs allow heirloom dolls to be displayed prominently and encourage children to become involved in creative play with their small counterparts.

Seating arrangements for dolls are as unique and varied as they are for the dolls' human handlers. With a little bit of effort, almost any adult-sized chair can be duplicated on a smaller scale for an 18" doll. Here in this chapter you will find four varieties of chairs: a rocking chair, a dining chair, an Adirondack chair and an old-fashioned chair desk.

When making chairs give intensive effort to accurately cutting the individual pieces to the dimensions indicated on the drawings. Many of the chair pieces are joined together with mortise and tendon joints. Accurately cut and fitted pieces are required for a strong joint because the glue is the only thing holding the assembly together. Mortise and tendon joints are precisely made using a mortising tool found in home centers. This inexpensive mortising attachment for a drill press was used in making the chairs in this book.

# Rocking Chair

## Materials List

| Item | Width | Length | Thickness | Quantity | Wood Type | Location |
|---|---|---|---|---|---|---|
| Left Leg | 2¼" | 12⅜" | ½" | 1 | Walnut | Page 23 |
| Right Leg | 2¼" | 12⅜" | ½" | 1 | Walnut | Page 22 |
| Rocker | 2¾" | 11½" | ¾" | 2 | Walnut | Page 24 |
| Left Front Leg | ½" | 7" | ½" | 1 | Walnut | Page 18 |
| Right Front Leg | ½" | 7" | ½" | 1 | Walnut | Page 18 |
| Arm Support | ½" | 5⅛" | ½" | 2 | Walnut | Page 18 |
| Arm | ¾" | 5¾" | ¾" | 2 | Walnut | Page 20 |
| Side Stretcher | 1" | 4⅜" | ⅜" | 2 | Walnut | Page 20 |
| Front Stretcher | 1" | 6" | 1" | 1 | Walnut | Page 19 |
| Back Stretcher | ¾" | 6" | ½" | 1 | Walnut | Page 19 |
| Splat | 1½" | 7¼" | ⅜" | 1 | Walnut | Page 21 |
| Back | 3" | 6¾" | ⅜" | 1 | Walnut | Page 21 |
| Seat | 5" | 6⅜" | ⅜" | 1 | Walnut | Page 25 |

# Construction Sequence: Rocking Chair

## Making the Legs

1. Select hardwood materials of the proper thickness for each chair part.
2. Cut the Left Front Leg and the Right Front Leg to the sizes specified on the drawings.
3. Photocopy the drawings for the Left Leg and the Right Leg. Use temporary adhesive to attach the photocopy to the wood selected for these pieces. Ensure that the straight edge of the photocopy is aligned with the edge of the board. Cut the angle cuts and leave the remainder of the board attached to the Left Leg and the Right Leg, as shown on the drawing.

### Technical Note:

The Legs must remain attached to the wood pieces until after the mortises have been cut in the Leg pieces.

4. Lay out the locations of the mortises specified on the drawings for the Left Front Leg, the Left Leg, the Right Front Leg and the Right Leg.
5. Use a ¼" mortise drill and cut all mortises ⅜" deep and to the length specified on the drawings.

## Making the Back

6. Photocopy the pattern for the Splat. Use temporary adhesive to attach the photocopy to the wood selected for the Splat.
7. Cut the materials to make the Splat and the Back Stretcher.
8. Lay out the locations of the mortises on the edge of these pieces as specified on the drawings.
9. Use a ¼" mortise drill and cut the mortises ⅜" deep and to the length specified on the drawings.
10. Lay out and cut the tenons on both ends of these pieces to the dimensions specified on the drawings.
11. Cut the decorative top profile on the Splat, following the lines on the photocopy.

12. Cut a piece of wood for the Back to the size specified on the drawing.
13. Photocopy the drawing for the Back. Use temporary adhesive to attach the photocopy to the wood selected for the Back.
14. Lay out and cut the tenons on both ends of these pieces to the dimensions specified on the drawing.
15. Drill pilot holes for the blade and use a scroll saw to cut the decorative profile for the Back.
16. Dry fit the Back with the Splat and the Back Stretcher. Dry fit the Back Assembly with the Left Leg and the Right Leg.
17. Apply glue to the tenons on the Back and to the mortises in the Splat and in the Back Stretcher. Clamp the Back Assembly, ensuring the assembly is square.

## Making the Stretchers

18. Cut the Arm Supports, the Side Stretchers and the Front Stretchers to the sizes specified on the drawings.
19. Lay out and cut the tenons on both ends of these pieces to the dimensions specified on the drawings.
20. Photocopy the pattern for the Side Stretcher and the Front Stretcher pieces. Use temporary adhesive to attach the photocopy to these pieces.
21. Cut the decorative profile on the bottom edges of the Side Stretchers and the Front Stretcher.
22. Dry assemble all the Stretcher pieces with the Legs made above. Ensure that all the tenons fit the mortises in the legs.

## Making the Chair Assembly

23. Apply glue to the tenons on the Front Stretcher and to the mortises in the Left Front Leg and the Right Front Leg and clamp. Ensure that the assembly is square and that the unused mortises on the Front Legs are oriented in the same direction.
24. Apply glue to the tenons on the Splat, the Back Stretcher and the Front Stretcher. Apply glue to the mortises in the Left Leg and the Right Leg.
25. Clamp the Back Leg Assembly together, ensuring that the assembly is square.
26. Apply glue to the tenons on the Side Stretchers, the Arm Supports and the mortises in the Leg Assemblies. Clamp the Chair Assembly together, ensuring that the assembly is square.
27. Photocopy the pattern for the Seat. Use temporary adhesive to attach the photocopy.
28. Cut the Seat to the size specified on the drawing and cut the notches in the Seat for the Legs.
29. Dry fit the Seat with the Chair Assembly.
30. Use a file and a sanding block to round over the front edge of the Seat, as shown on the drawing.
31. Apply glue to the top edge of the Stretchers and clamp the Seat to the Chair Assembly.
32. Photocopy the drawing for the Arm pieces. Use temporary adhesive to attach the photocopy to the wood selected for the Arms.
33. Cut the decorative profile for the Arms using a scroll saw.
34. Glue and clamp the Arms to the Arm Supports.

## Making the Rockers

35. Photocopy the drawing for the Rockers. Use temporary adhesive to attach the photocopy to the wood selected for the Rockers. Ensure that the straight edge of the photocopy is aligned with the edge of the wood piece.
36. Cut the decorative profile on the topside of the Rockers.
37. Cut the 22-degree angle cut and leave the Rockers attached to the remainder of the boards, as shown on the drawing.
38. Lay out the locations of the mortises shown on the drawing to match the tenons on the assembled chair.

**Technical Note:**

The Rockers must remain attached to the wood pieces until after the mortises have been cut.

39. Use a ¼" mortise drill and cut the mortises ⅜" deep and to the length specified on the drawing.

**Technical Note:**

The mortise locations shown on the Rocker drawing indicate the proper location for the mortises if all of the chair's components are made precisely as specified on the drawings. Any variation in component sizes could result in a mismatched fit with the Rockers. It is best to lay the assembled rocking chair along-side the Rockers to compare the tenons on the chair with the mortise locations on the photocopy. Re-mark the mortise locations as needed to fit with the assembled chair.

40. Dry fit the assembled rocking chair with the Rockers.
41. Cut the decorative profile on the bottom side of the Rockers.
42. Glue and clamp the Rockers to the Chair Assembly.

## Finishing
43. Sand the assembled rocking chair and apply a finish.

CHAIRS

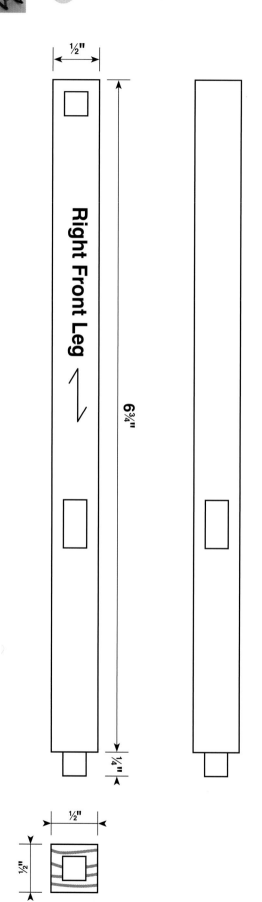

**Right Front Leg** ➚

½"

6¾"

¼"

½"

½"

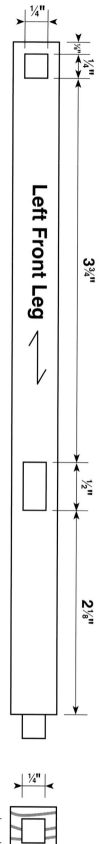

**Left Front Leg** ➚

¼"

⅛"

¼"

3¾"

½"

2⅛"

¼"

¼"

¼"

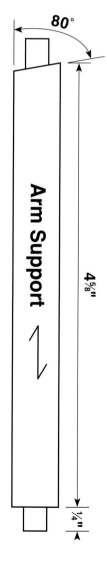

80°

**Arm Support** ➚

4⅝"

¼"

Shown actual size.

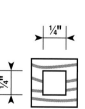

CHAIRS

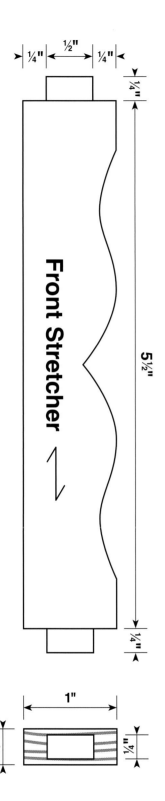

¼" ½" ¼"

¼"

**Front Stretcher** →

5½"

¼"

1"

⅜" ¼"

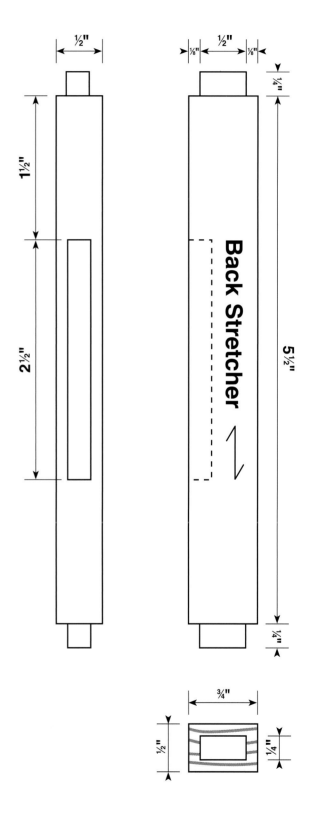

½"

1½"

2½"

½"

⅛" ½" ⅛"

¼"

**Back Stretcher** →

5½"

¼"

¾"

½" ¼"

Shown actual size.

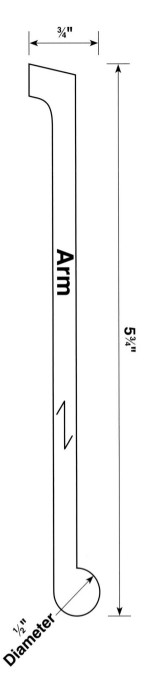

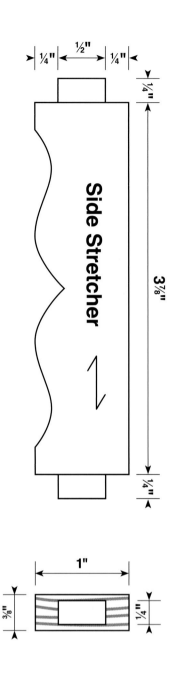

Shown actual size.

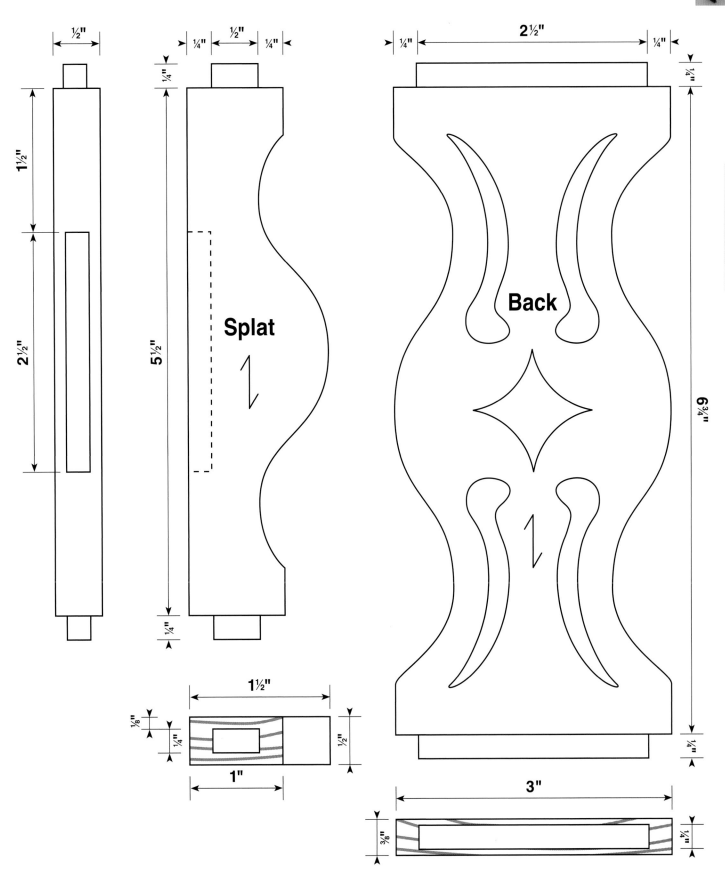

½"

¼" ½" ¼"

¼" 2½" ¼"

¼"

1½"

¼"

5½"

2½"

**Splat**

**Back**

6¾"

¼"

¼"

1½"

⅛"

¼"

½"

1"

3"

⅜"

¼"

Shown actual size.

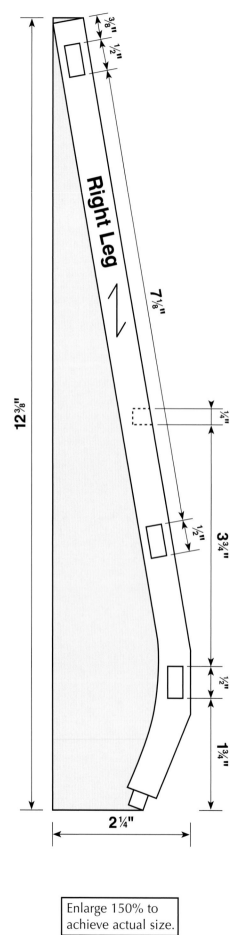

**Right Leg**

3/8"

1/2"

7 1/8"

12 3/8"

1/4"

1/2"

3 3/4"

1/2"

1 1/4"

2 1/4"

Enlarge 150% to
achieve actual size.

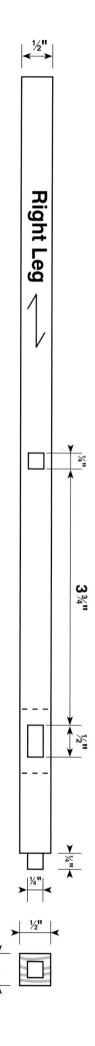

1/2"

**Right Leg**

1/4"

3 3/4"

1/2"

1/4"

1/4"

1/2"

1/2"

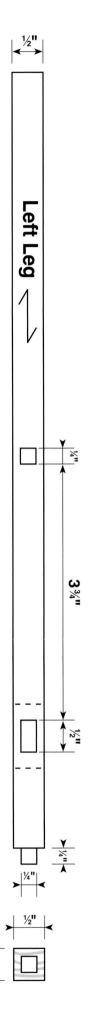

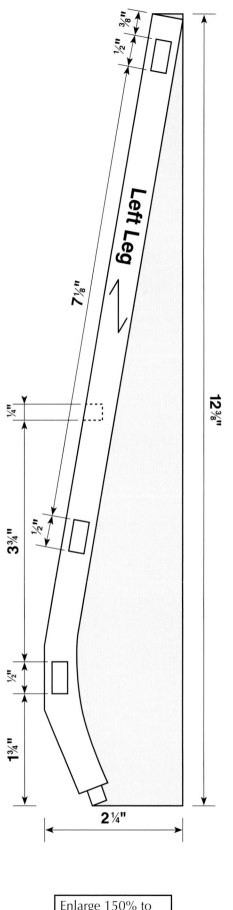

Enlarge 150% to
achieve actual size.

2¾"

20°

11½"

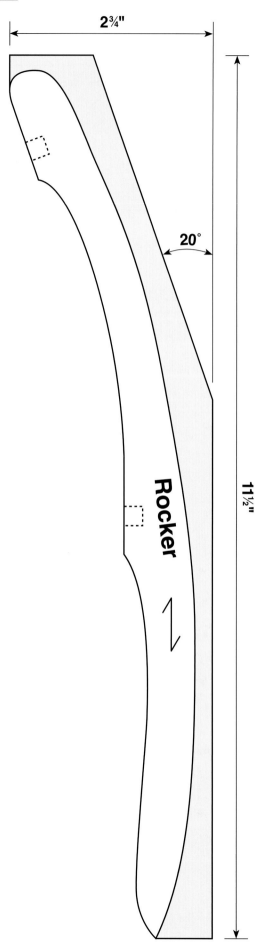

**Rocker**

Enlarge 125% to achieve actual size.

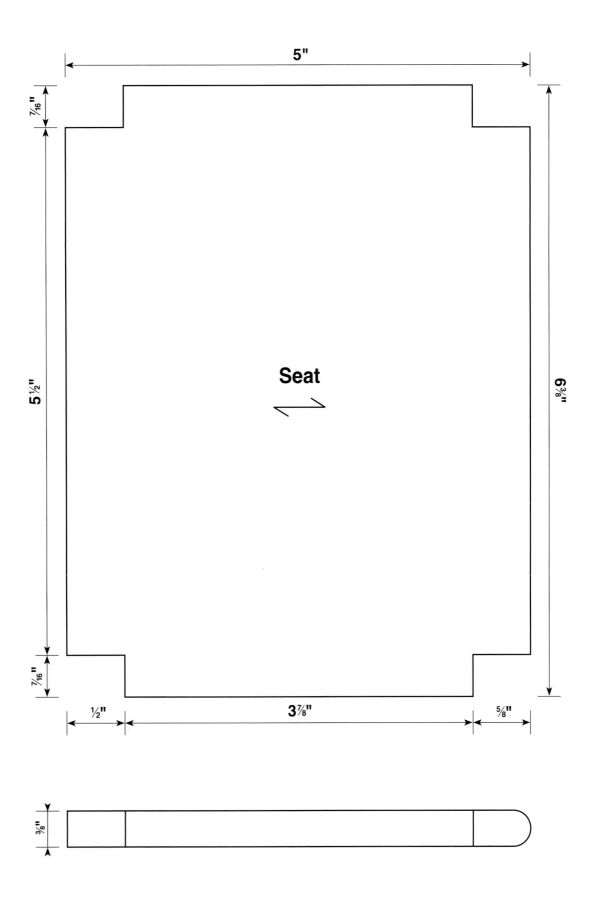

5"

7/16"

5½"

6⅜"

**Seat**

7/16"

½"    3⅞"    ⅝"

⅜"

Shown actual size.

# Dining Chair

## Materials List

| Item | Width | Length | Thickness | Quantity | Wood Type | Location |
|---|---|---|---|---|---|---|
| Left Leg | 2" | 11½" | ½" | 1 | Cherry | Page 32 |
| Right Leg | 2" | 11½" | ½" | 1 | Cherry | Page 32 |
| Front Leg | ½" | 4⅜" | ½" | 2 | Cherry | Page 31 |
| Upper Stretcher | ¾" | 5¼" | ⅜" | 2 | Cherry | Page 29 |
| Lower Stretcher | ⅝" | 5¼" | ⅜" | 2 | Cherry | Page 29 |
| Back Stretcher | ¾" | 5¼" | ⅜" | 1 | Cherry | Page 29 |
| Back Slat | ⅝" | 4" | ⅛" | 4 | Cherry | Page 30 |
| Splat | 1¼" | 5¼" | ⅜" | 1 | Cherry | Page 29 |
| Upper Side Stretcher | ¾" | 4½" | ⅜" | 2 | Cherry | Page 31 |
| Lower Side Stretcher | ⅝" | 4½" | ⅜" | 2 | Cherry | Page 31 |
| Seat | 5⅛" | 5⅞" | ⅜" | 1 | Cherry | Page 30 |

CHAIRS

# Construction Sequence: Dining Chair

## Making the Legs

1. Select hardwood materials of the proper thickness for each chair part.
2. Cut the Front Legs to the size specified on the drawing.
3. Photocopy the drawings for the Left Leg and the Right Leg pieces. Use temporary adhesive to attach the photocopy to the wood. Ensure that the straight edge of the photocopy is aligned with the edge of the wood piece. Cut the angle cuts and leave the remainder of the boards attached to the Legs as shown on the drawings.

### Technical Note:

The Legs must remain attached to the wood pieces until after the mortises have been cut in the Leg pieces.

## Making the Splat and the Stretchers

4. Cut the materials to make the Splat and the Back Stretcher.

### Technical Note:

Stretcher pieces have a dado groove cut in the edge. These pieces are too small to handle safely when cutting the dado. Cut the dado in an oversized board before cutting the pieces to their final widths and lengths. This improves the safety of the dado operation.

## The Splat and the Back

5. Cut a ⅛" x ⅛" dado groove on the edges of the boards for the Splat and the Back Stretcher pieces.
6. Lay out and cut the tenons on both ends of these pieces to the dimensions specified on the drawings.

7. Photocopy the pattern for the Splat. Use temporary adhesive to attach the photocopied pattern; then cut the rounded top profile on the Splat.

8. Cut the Upper and Lower Stretchers and the Upper and Lower Side Stretchers to the sizes specified.z

9. Lay out and cut the tenons on both ends of these pieces to the dimensions specified on the drawings.

10. Cut the Back Slats to the size specified on the drawing.

11. Cut ten pieces of wood ⅛"x 1⅛" and ⅜" long. Glue these into the dado groove in the Splat and the Back Stretcher. These pieces act as spacers and fill in the dado groove between the Back Slats.

12. Glue and clamp these spacers to the Splat and the Back Stretcher.

## Making the Chair Assembly

13. Dry assemble all the Stretcher pieces with the Legs made above. Ensure that all of the tenons fit all of the mortises in the Legs.

14. Apply glue to the tenons on the Upper Stretchers and the Lower Stretchers and to the mortises in the two Front Legs. Clamp.

15. Ensure that the assembly is square and that the unused mortises on the Front Legs are oriented in the same direction.

16. Apply glue to the tenons on the Splat, the Back Stretcher and the Upper and Lower Stretchers. Apply glue to the mating mortises in the Left Leg and the Right Leg. Clamp the Back Leg Assembly together, ensuring that the assembly is square.

17. Apply glue to the tenons on the Upper and Lower Side Stretchers and the mortises in the Leg Assemblies. Clamp the Chair Assembly together, ensuring that the assembly is square.

18. Cut the Seat to the size specified on the drawing. Cut the notches in the Seat for the Left and Right Legs. Dry fit the Seat with the Chair Assembly.

19. Apply glue to the top edge of the Stretchers and clamp the Seat to the Chair Assembly.

## Finishing

20. Sand the chair and apply a finish.

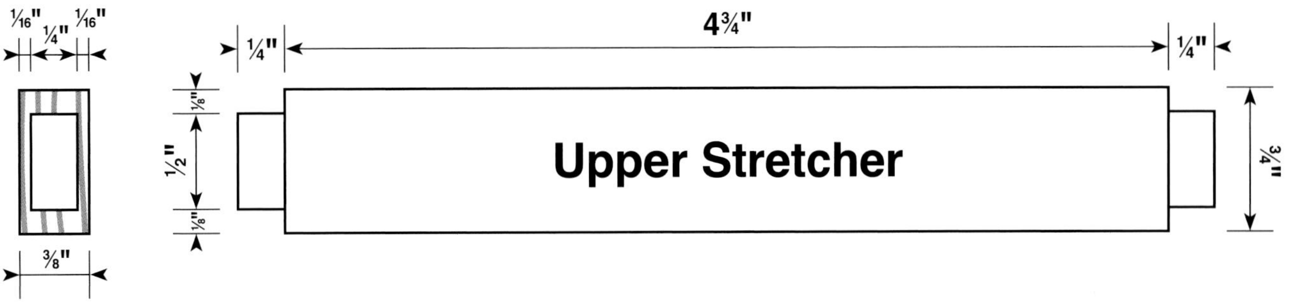
1/16"
1/4"
1/16"
3/8"
1/4"
4 3/4"
1/4"
1/8"
1/2"
1/8"
Upper Stretcher
3/4"

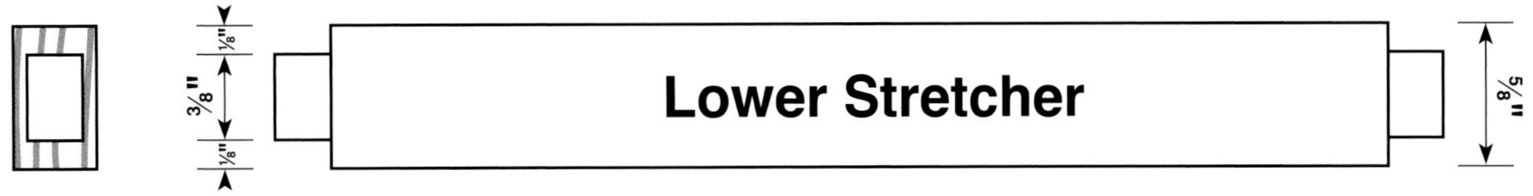
1/8"
3/8"
1/8"
Lower Stretcher
5/8"

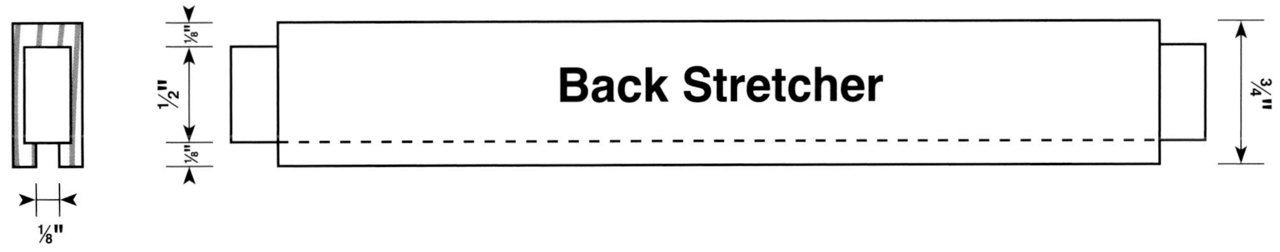
1/8"
1/8"
1/2"
1/8"
Back Stretcher
3/4"

Shown actual size.

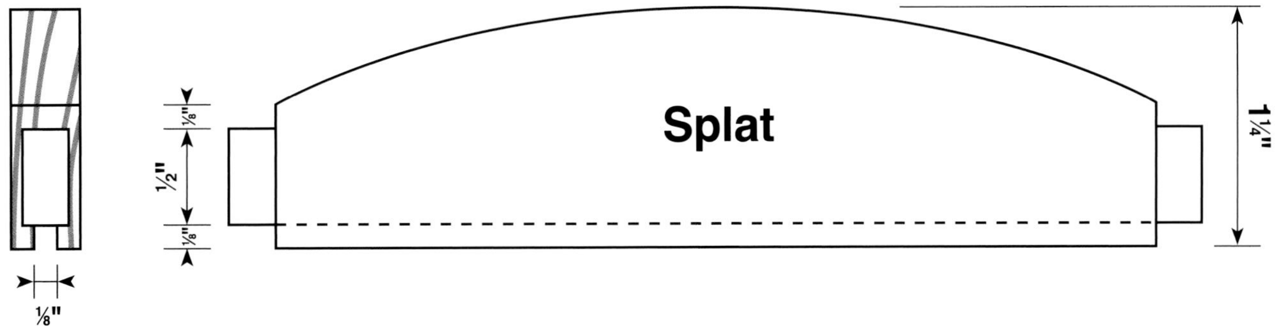
1/8"
1/8"
1/2"
1/8"
Splat
1 1/4"

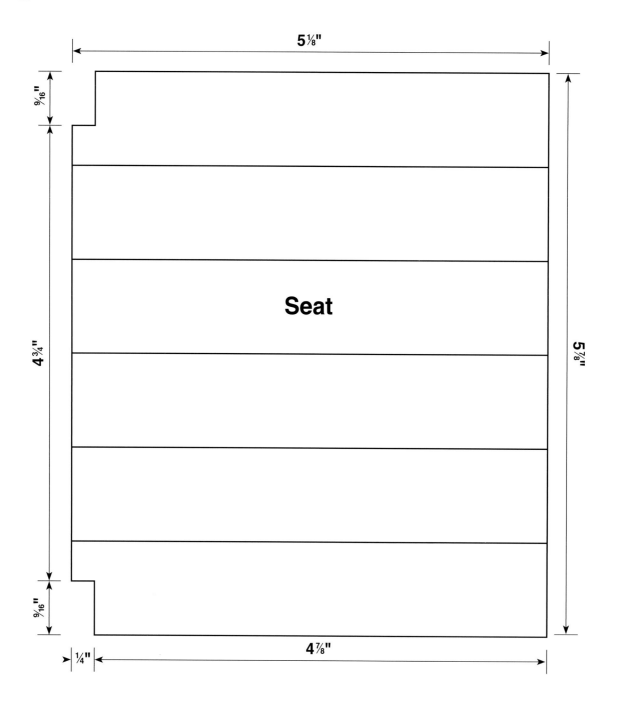

5⅛"

9/16"

4¾"

**Seat**

5⅞"

9/16"

4⅞"

¼"

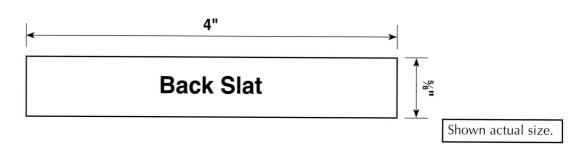

4"

**Back Slat**

⅝"

Shown actual size.

1/16"
1/4"
1/16"
3/8"
1/4"
4"
1/4"
1/8"
1/2"
1/8"
Upper Side Stretcher
3/4"

1/8"
3/8"
1/8"
Lower Side Stretcher
5/8"

4 3/8"
Front Leg
1/2"
1/4"
2"
3/8"
1 3/8"
1/2"
1/8"

Shown actual size.

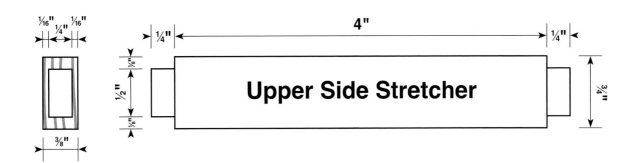

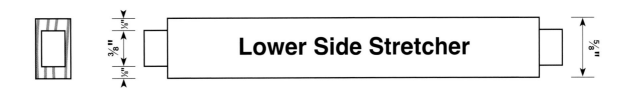

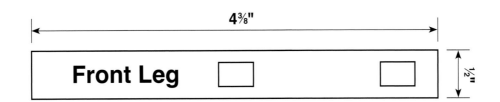

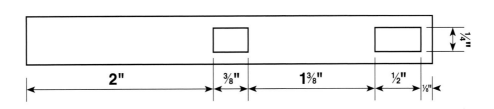

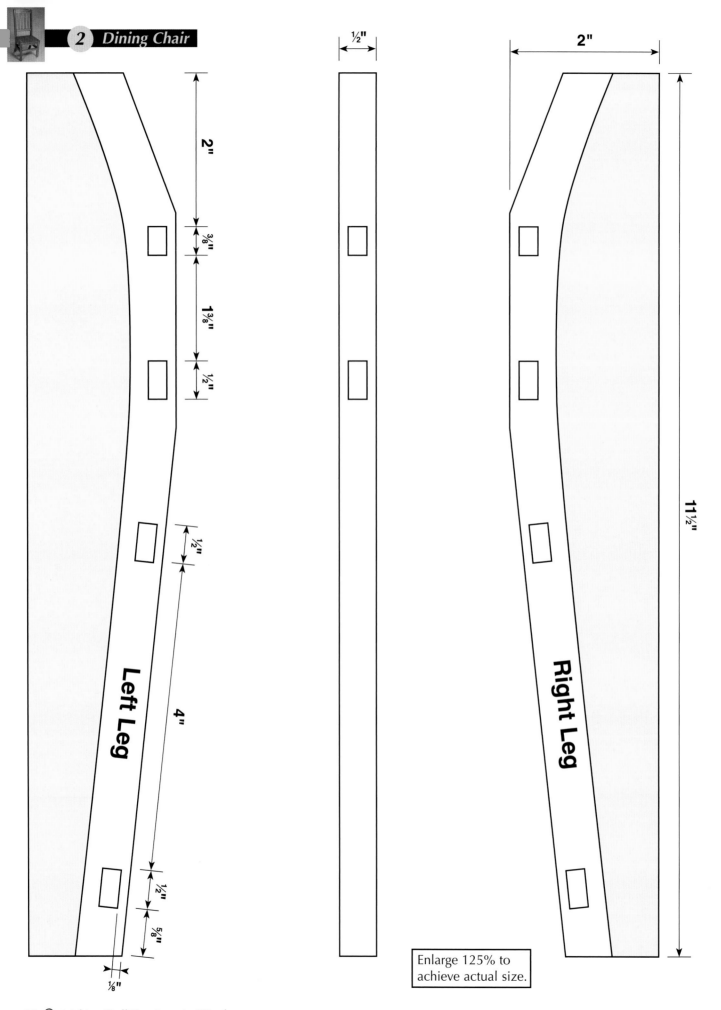

2"

½"

2"

3/8"

1 3/8"

½"

½"

11½"

4"

**Left Leg**

**Right Leg**

½"

5/8"

1/8"

Enlarge 125% to
achieve actual size.

# *Adirondack Chair*

## Materials List

| Item | Width | Length | Thickness | Quantity | Wood Type | Location |
|------|-------|--------|-----------|----------|-----------|----------|
| Leg | 7/8" | 11¼" | 3/8" | 2 | Poplar | Page 37 |
| Back | 6" | 11" | ¼" | 1 | Poplar | Page 36 |
| Seat Slat | ½" | 6⅞" | ¼" | 10 | Poplar | Page 38 |
| Rear Slat | 1¾" | 6⅞" | ¼" | 1 | Poplar | Page 38 |
| Arm | 1⅛" | 7⅞" | ¼" | 2 | Poplar | Page 38 |
| Front Leg | ¾" | 5¾" | 3/8" | 2 | Poplar | No drawing |
| Back Bow | 1¾" | 6⅞" | 3/8" | 3 | Poplar | Page 38 |
| Assembly Template | 1¾" | 7¾" | 3/8" | 1 | Poplar | Page 37 |

# Construction Sequence: Adirondack Chair

1. Select wood of the proper thickness for each chair part. Select wood with a fine grain that is in scale with the furniture being built.
2. Photocopy the drawing for the Legs. Use temporary adhesive to attach the photocopy to the wood selected for the Legs and cut out the two Legs.
3. Cut the Front Legs and the Seat Slats to the sizes specified on the drawings.
4. Photocopy the drawings for the Rear Slat, the Arm and the Back Bow pieces. Use temporary adhesive to attach these photocopies to the wood. Cut out each piece.
5. Photocopy the drawing for the Back. Use temporary adhesive to attach the photocopy to the wood selected for the Back. Then cut the profile for the Back.
6. Cut the Back into individual slats by cutting on the slat lines as indicated on the drawing.

> **Technical Note:**
>
> Lay out the Back pieces in the order they were cut. Take the outer two pieces from the set and reverse sides. Do the same with the pair on both sides of the centerpiece. Mixing these pieces changes the grain pattern and makes the assembly look like it was made from separate pieces of wood.

7. Start at the front of the Legs and glue and clamp the Seat Slats to the two Legs.
8. Ensure that the Seat Slats are flush with the sides of the Legs and that the assembly is square.
9. Glue and clamp the Rear Slat to the assembly.
10. Glue and clamp the Front Legs to each side of the assembly. The Front Legs will be set back from the front end of the assembly by 1½" and extend 1¼" below the assembly. Ensure that the Front Legs are square with the workbench top when they are placed in the normal use position.

> **Technical Note:**
>
> Adding the Front Legs to the assembly above can be easier if an Assembly Template is used. Make the Template by cutting a triangle from scrap wood. The Template will help align the Front Legs to the assembly.

11. Glue and clamp one of the Back Bow cutouts to the bottom edges of the Back pieces. Ensure that these pieces are square to the Back Bow.
12. Glue and clamp the Back Assembly into position with the Chair Leg Assembly.
13. Place the Chair Assembly on the workbench top with the chair in the upright position.
14. Clamp the Arms and the center Back Bow to the Chair Assembly. Ensure that the Arms will be 5¾" up the bench top. Mark the location where the center Back Bow should be glued to the Back Assembly.

### Technical Note:

The angle of the Back Bow (when clamped to the Back Assembly) and the angle of the Arms (when attached to the Front Legs) do not fit together correctly. The ends of this Back Bow piece will need a small angle cut where the Arms attach. These small angle cuts are not shown on the drawing.

15. Glue and clamp the center Back Bow to the Back Assembly.
16. Glue and clamp the top Back Bow to the Back Assembly near the top of the assembly.
17. Glue and clamp the Arms to the center Back Bow and the Front Legs. Small finish brad nails could be used to strengthen the connection of the Arms to the Front Legs.
18. Sand the chair and apply a finish.

CHAIRS

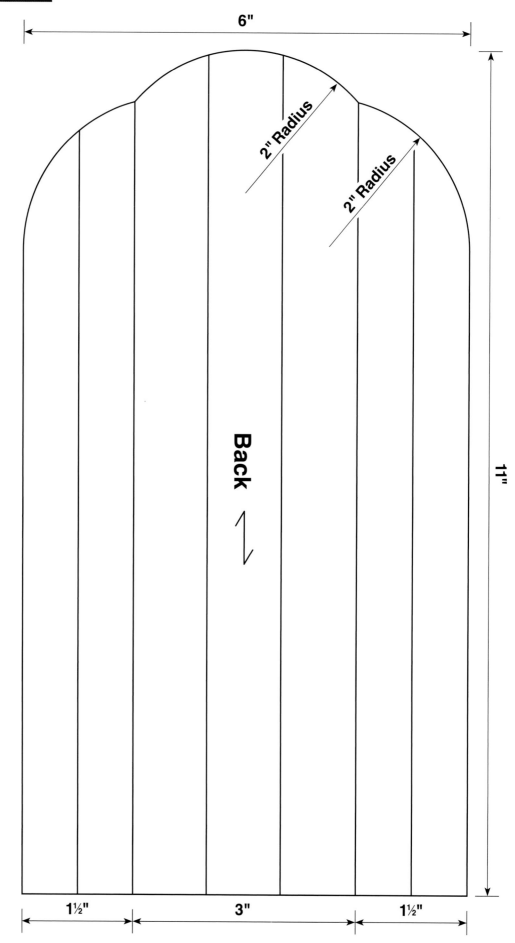

6"

2" Radius

2" Radius

**Back** ↗

11"

Enlarge 125% to achieve actual size.

1½"

3"

1½"

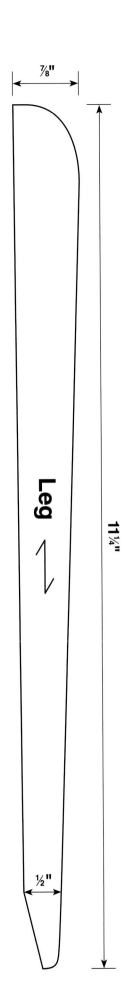

7⁄8"

**Leg**

11¼"

½"

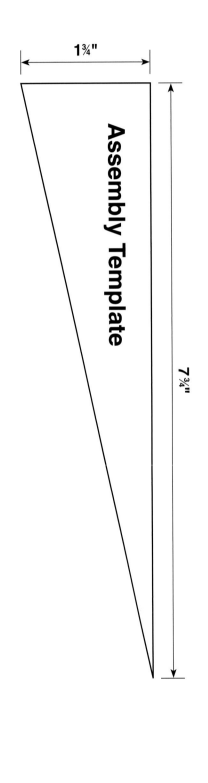

1¾"

**Assembly Template**

7¾"

Enlarge 125% to achieve actual size.

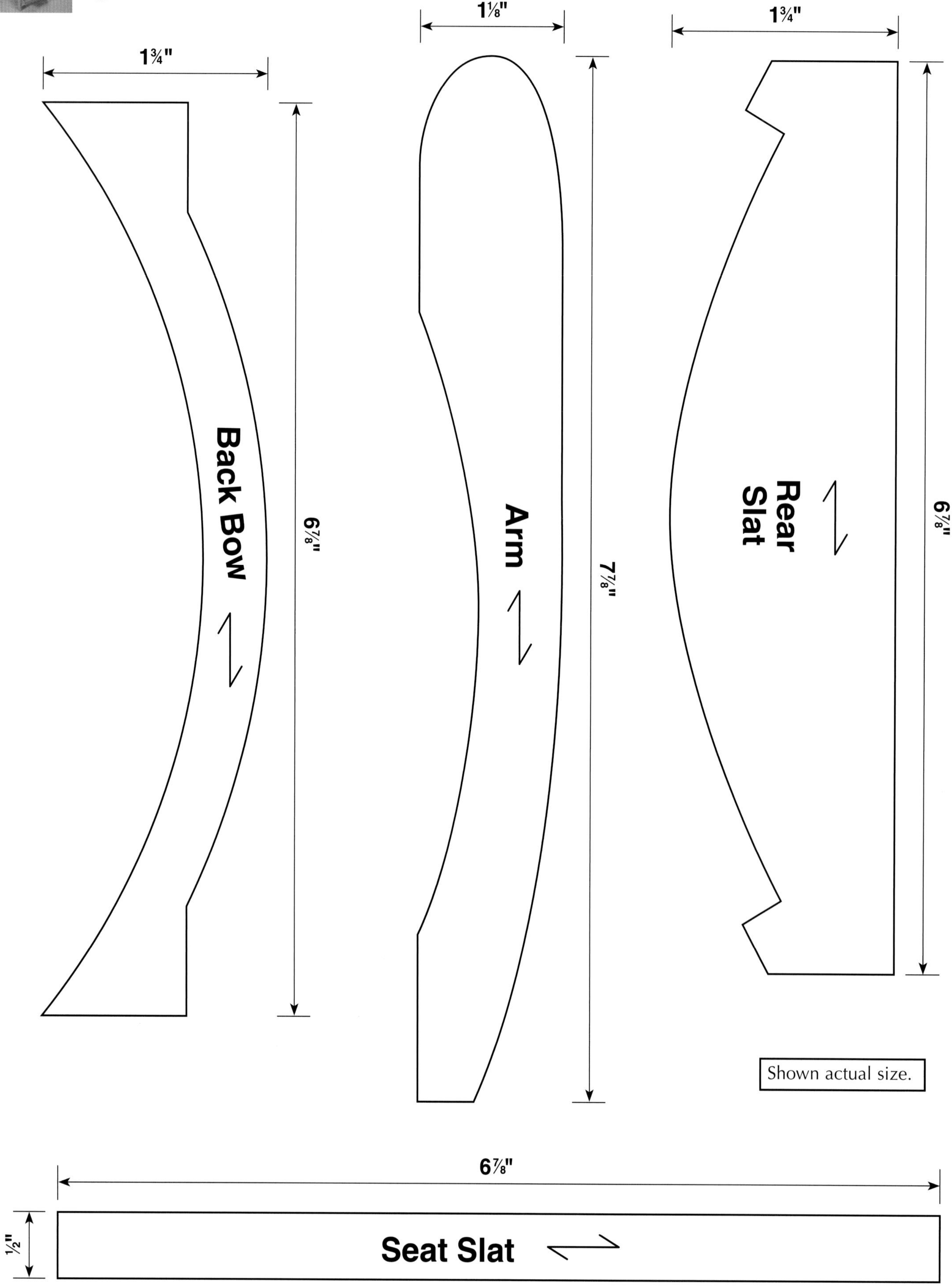

1¾"

1⅛"

1¾"

**Back Bow** →

6⅞"

**Arm** →

7⅞"

**Rear Slat** →

6⅞"

Shown actual size.

6⅞"

½"

**Seat Slat** →

# *Chair Desk*

## Materials List

| Item | Width | Length | Thickness | Quantity | Wood Type | Location |
|---|---|---|---|---|---|---|
| Left Leg | 1½" | 9¾" | ½" | 1 | Birch | Page 44 |
| Right Leg | 1½" | 9¾" | ½" | 1 | Birch | Page 44 |
| Arm Leg | ½" | 6⅝" | ½" | 1 | Birch | Page 43 |
| Front Leg | ½" | 4⅛" | ½" | 1 | Birch | Page 43 |
| Upper Stretcher & Slat | ¾" | 5¾" | ⅜" | 5 | Birch | Page 42 |
| Lower Stretcher | ½" | 5¾" | ⅜" | 2 | Birch | Page 42 |
| Top Side Stretcher | ¾" | 4½" | ⅜" | 2 | Birch | Page 42 |
| Bottom Side Stretcher | ½" | 4½" | ⅜" | 2 | Birch | Page 42 |
| Arm Support | ½" | 4¹³⁄₁₆" | ½" | 1 | Birch | Page 45 |
| Top Support | 1½" | 1½" | ½" | 1 | Birch | Page 45 |
| Desk Top | 4" | 8" | ⅜" | 1 | Birch | Page 45 |
| Seat | 5⅜" | 6⅝" | ⅜" | 1 | Birch | Page 46 |

# Construction Sequence: Chair Desk

## Making the Legs

1. Select hardwood materials of the proper thickness for each chair part.
2. Cut the Arm Leg and the Front Leg to the sizes specified on the drawings.
3. Photocopy the drawings for the Left Leg and the Right Leg pieces. Use temporary adhesive to attach the photocopy to the wood. Ensure that the straight edge of the photocopy is aligned with the edge of the wood piece. Cut the angle cuts and leave the remainder of the boards attached to the Legs, as shown on the drawing.

### Technical Note:

The Legs must remain attached to the wood pieces until after the mortises have been cut in the Leg pieces.

4. Lay out the locations of the mortises specified on the drawings for the Arm Leg, the Front Leg, the Left Leg and the Right Leg. Note: The mortise for the Arm Support is only cut in the Left Leg.
5. Use a ¼" mortise drill and cut all mortises ⅜" deep and to the lengths specified on the drawings.

## Making the Chair Assembly

6. Cut the materials to the sizes specified on the drawings to make the Arm Support, the Top Side Stretcher, the Bottom Side Stretcher, the Lower Stretcher, the Upper Stretcher and the Slat pieces.
7. Lay out and cut the tenons on both ends of these pieces to the dimensions specified on the drawings.

8. Dry assemble all the Stretcher pieces with the Legs made above. Ensure that all tenons fit the mortises in the Legs.
9. Apply glue to the tenons on one Upper Stretcher & Slat and one Lower Stretcher. Apply glue to the mortises in the Arm Leg and the Front Leg. Ensure that the assembly is square and that the unused mortises on the Arm Leg and the Front Leg are oriented in the same direction.
10. Apply glue to the tenons on the four remaining Upper Stretcher & Slat pieces and one Lower Stretcher. Apply glue to the mortises in the Left and the Right Legs. Clamp the Back Leg Assembly together, ensuring that the assembly is square.
11. Apply glue to the tenons on the two Top Side Stretchers, the two Bottom Side Stretchers and the Arm Support, and to the mortises in the Leg Assemblies. Clamp the Chair Assembly together, ensuring that the assembly is square.

## Making the Seat

12. Photocopy the drawing for the Seat. Use temporary adhesive to attach the photocopy to the wood selected for the Seat.
13. Cut the Seat to the size specified on the drawing. Cut the notches in the Seat for the Arm Leg, the Left Leg and the Right Leg. Dry fit the Seat with the Chair Assembly.
14. Apply glue to the top edge of the Stretchers and clamp the Seat to the Chair Assembly.

## Making the Arm Support and the Desk Top

15. Cut the Arm Support to the size specified on the drawing.
16. Cut the tenon on the Arm Support to the size specified on the drawing.
17. Apply glue and clamp the Arm Support to the Arm Leg.
18. Photocopy the drawing for the Desk Top. Use temporary adhesive to attach the photocopy to the wood selected for the Desk Top. Cut out the Desk Top, following the lines on the drawing.
19. Apply glue to the top surface of the Arm Support and the Top Support. Clamp the Desk Top to the Chair Assembly.

## Finishing

20. Sand the chair and apply a finish.

CHAIRS

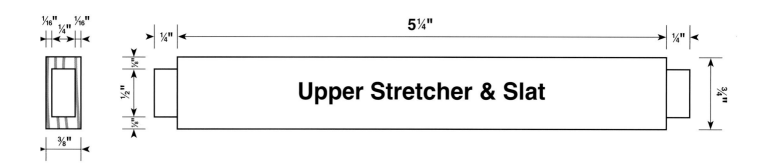

**Upper Stretcher & Slat**

5¼"

**Lower Stretcher**

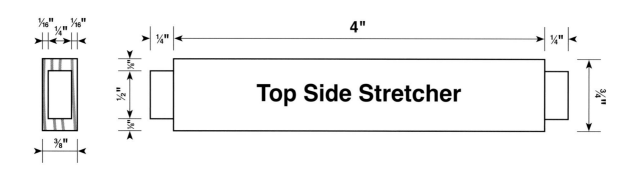

4"

**Top Side Stretcher**

**Bottom Side Stretcher**

Shown actual size.

4⅛"

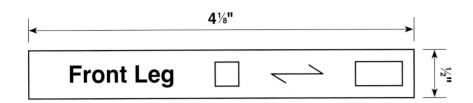

**Front Leg**

½"

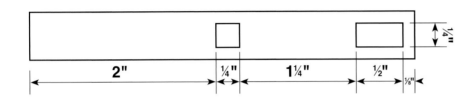

¼"

2"          ¼"      1¼"        ½"    ⅛"

7"

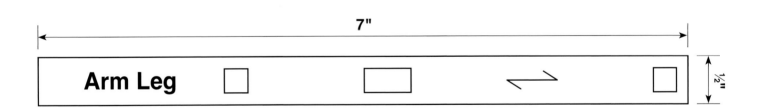

**Arm Leg**

½"

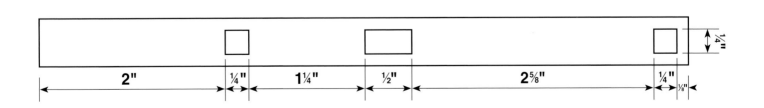

¼"

2"          ¼"      1¼"        ½"          2⅝"            ¼"  ⅛"

Shown actual size.

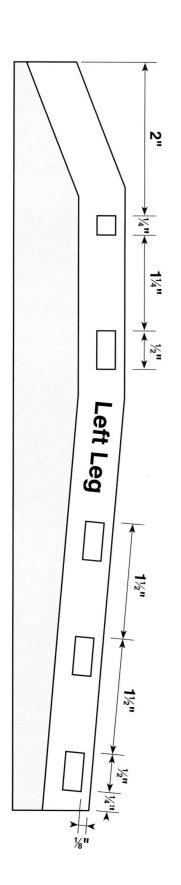

**Left Leg**

2"

¼"

1¼"

½"

1½"

1½"

½"

¼"

⅛"

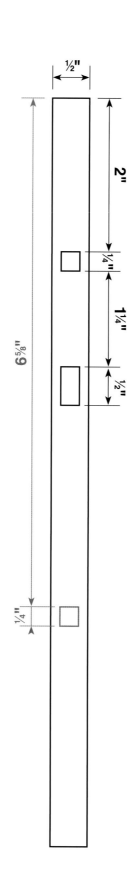

½"

2"

¼"

1¼"

½"

9⅝"

¼"

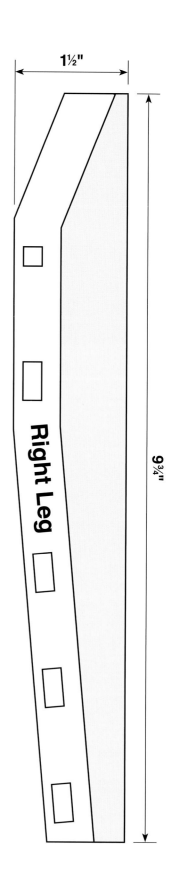

**Right Leg**

1½"

9¾"

Enlarge 125% to
achieve actual size.

CHAIRS

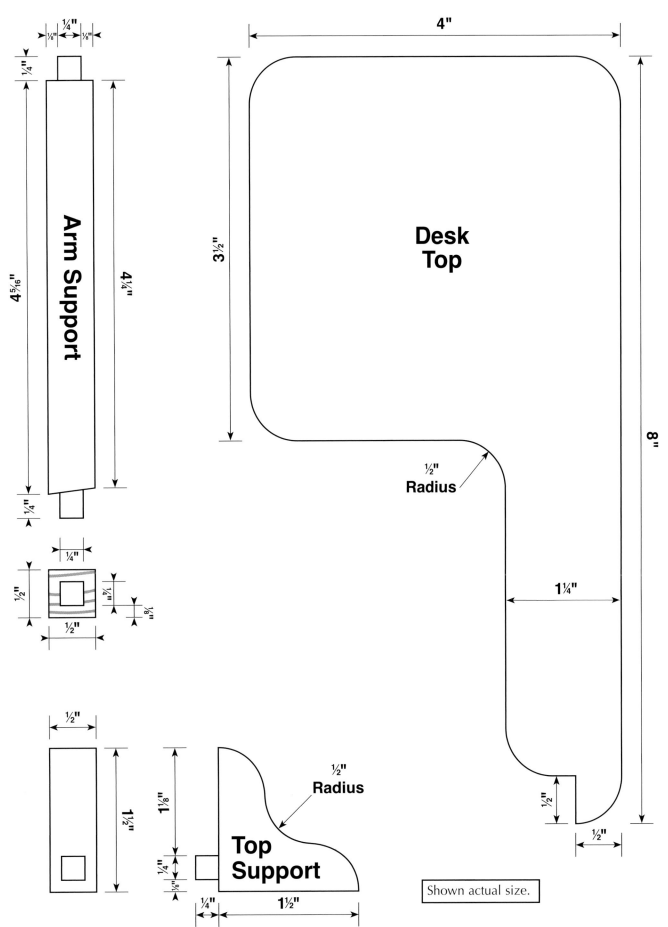

**Arm Support**

4⁵⁄₁₆"

4¼"

¼"

⅛" ¼" ⅛"

¼"

¼"

½"

½"

¼"

¼"

⅛"

4"

3½"

**Desk Top**

½"
Radius

1¼"

8"

½"

½"

½"

1½"

1⅛"

1"

¼"

⅛"

½"
Radius

**Top Support**

¼"

1½"

Shown actual size.

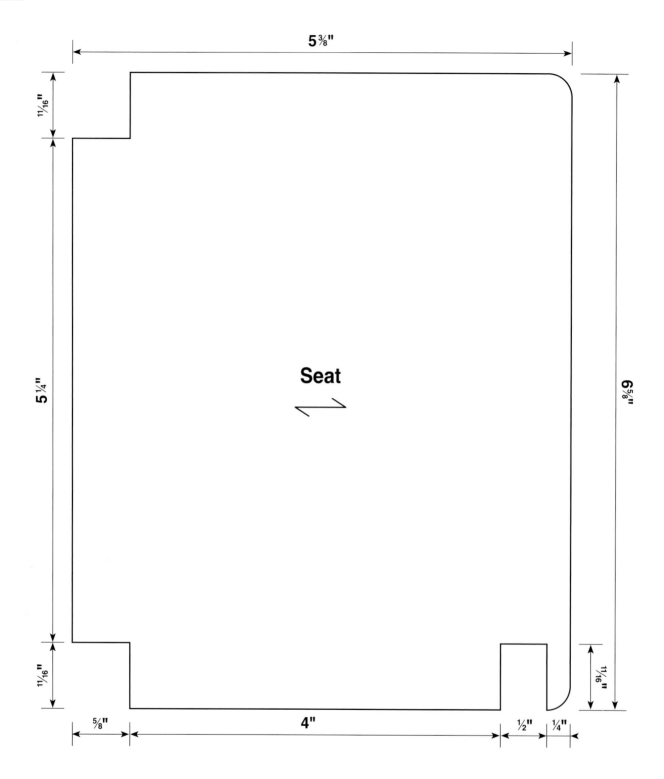

5⅜"

11/16"

5¼"

6⅝"

**Seat**

11/16"

11/16"

⅝"

4"

½"

¼"

Shown actual size.

# Part Three

# *Doll*
# *Tables*

*Page 48*

O f course, once you have a chair for your doll, you'll want to make a matching table to make a set. While tables are a great addition to a display of cherished dolls, they are an even greater asset to a child's collection of dolls and doll accessories. A table is an open invitation for a child to gather more dolls for play at a tea party or for an afternoon of fun at an outdoor picnic.

Here in this section you will find four table projects: an Adirondack table, a dining table, a picnic table and a Southwestern-style nightstand. The Adirondack table and the dining table are perfect matches for the Adirondack chair and the dining chair in the previous section. The picnic table is a stand-alone piece. The Southwestern-style nightstand will be matched up with a bed in Part Four.

When making tables the grain pattern of the wood becomes visible in the tabletop. I recommend using a tight-grained hardwood with narrow grain lines. Gluing narrow boards together will make the tabletop look more authentic and to scale for doll size furniture.

*Page 51*

*Page 56*

*Page 60*

# *Adirondack Table*

## Materials List

| Item | Width | Length | Thickness | Quantity | Wood Type | Location |
|---|---|---|---|---|---|---|
| Top | ½" | 4½" | ¼" | 8 | Fine grain pine | Page 50 |
| Foot & Support | ½" | 4" | ¼" | 4 | Fine grain pine | Page 50 |
| Leg | 1" | 5" | ¼" | 4 | Fine grain pine | Page 50 |
| Stretcher | ½" | 3¼" | ¼" | 2 | Fine grain pine | Page 50 |

# Construction Sequence: Adirondack Table

1. Select wood materials of the proper thickness for each part. Select wood with fine grain lines that are in scale with this piece of furniture.
2. Lay out and cut all the pieces to the sizes specified on the drawings.
3. Lay the eight Top pieces together in alignment, bottom sides up. Mark a line ⅜" from each end of the Top pieces. These lines represent the locations where two of the Foot & Support pieces attach to the Top pieces.
4. Glue and clamp the two Foot & Support pieces to the Top.
5. Fit and glue the two Stretchers ¾" in from each edge of the assembled Top and between the two Foot & Support pieces.
6. Glue and clamp two of the Leg pieces to each of the Foot & Support pieces. Ensure that these pieces are square with the assembled Top.
7. Glue and clamp the remaining two Leg pieces to the other end of the Top Assembly.
8. Glue and clamp the Foot & Support pieces and the Stretcher pieces to the bottom of each of the Legs. Ensure that these are spaced in a similar manner as the Top pieces.
9. Sand the table and apply a finish.

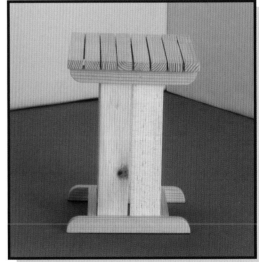

TABLES

5"

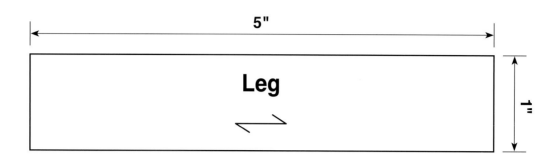

**Leg**

1"

3¼"

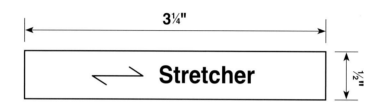

**Stretcher**

½"

4"

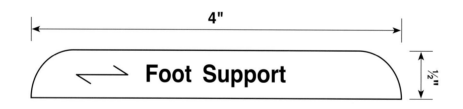

**Foot Support**

½"

4½"

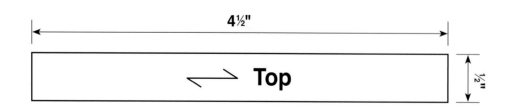

**Top**

½"

Shown actual size.

# Dining Table

## Materials List

| Item | Width | Length | Thickness | Quantity | Wood Type | Location |
|---|---|---|---|---|---|---|
| Top | 8½" | 13" | ¼" | 1 | Cherry | Page 55 |
| Sub-Top | 6⅜" | 10⅝" | ⅜" | 1 | Cherry | |
| Leg | ⅝" | 8½" | ⅝" | 4 | Cherry | Page 54 |
| Long Stretcher | 1" | 11" | ½" | 2 | Cherry | Page 54 |
| Short Stretcher | 1" | 6¾" | ½" | 2 | Cherry | Page 54 |

# Construction Sequence: Dining Table

## Making the Top

1. Select wood materials of the proper thickness for each part. Select wood with fine grain lines in scale with the furniture being built.
2. Lay out and cut nine Top pieces 1" wide and 13½" long to make the Top. Match these pieces for grain pattern and color.
3. Apply glue to the edges and clamp the Top Assembly.

## Making the Legs and the Stretchers

4. Cut materials for the four Legs to the size specified on the drawing.
5. Lay out the location of the mortises on the Legs and cut them as indicated on the drawing. Cut two ¼" x ½" mortises, ⅜" deep, in each Leg. Mortises are cut on two sides of the Legs, 90 degrees from each other.
6. Cut the materials for the Long Stretchers and the Short Stretchers.
7. Cut the tenons on both ends of the Stretcher pieces as specified on the drawings.
8. Dry fit the tenons on the Stretchers with the mortises in the Legs.
9. Apply glue to the tenons on the Short Stretchers and in the mortises in the Legs.
10. Assemble and clamp these pieces, ensuring that the assembly is square and that the unused mortises are facing the same direction.
11. Apply glue to the tenons on the Long Stretchers and in the mortises in the Legs.
12. Assemble and clamp these pieces, ensuring that the assembly is square.

## Making the Sub-Top

13. Cut a piece of wood to make the Sub-Top. This piece must fit snugly between the four Stretchers.

### Technical Note:

> The purpose of the Sub-Top is to strengthen the Leg and the Stretcher joint and provide additional contact surface to glue the Top to the Leg Assembly. The drawing dimensions are approximate. Adjust the dimensions to match the Leg Assembly made in the previous steps.

14. Apply glue to the edges of the Sub-Top and clamp it to the Leg Assembly. Ensure that the Sub-Top is flush to the top surface of Stretchers.

15. Apply glue to the top surface of the Sub-Top and clamp the Top to the assembly. Ensure that the Top is centered on the length and the width of the Leg Assembly.

## Finishing

16. Sand the table and apply a finish.

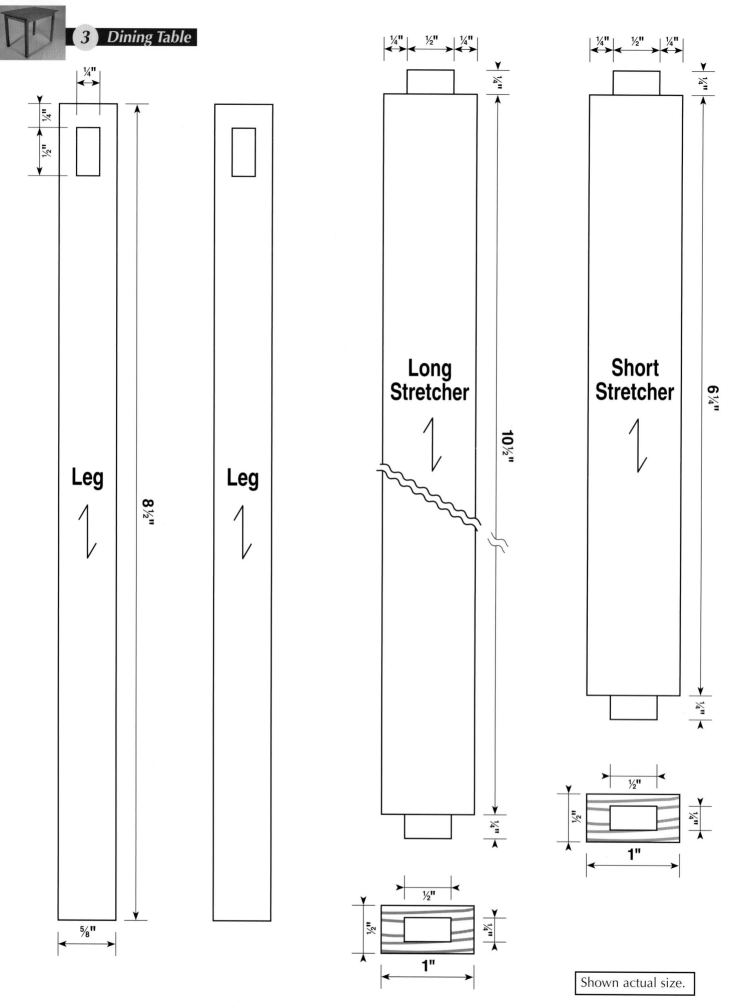

¼"

¼"

½"

Leg

8½"

5⁄8"

Leg

¼"  ½"  ¼"

¼"

Long
Stretcher

10½"

¼"

½"

½"

¼"

1"

¼"  ½"  ¼"

¼"

Short
Stretcher

6¼"

¼"

½"

½"

¼"

1"

Shown actual size.

13"

8½"

**Top**

Enlarge 200% to
achieve actual size.

# *Picnic Table*

## Materials List

| Item | Width | Length | Thickness | Quantity | Wood Type | Location |
|---|---|---|---|---|---|---|
| Leg | 1" | 9" | ³⁄₈" | 4 | Birch | Page 58 |
| Angle Brace | ⁵⁄₈" | 7" | ³⁄₈" | 2 | Birch | Page 58 |
| Top Support | 1" | 7" | ³⁄₈" | 2 | Birch | Page 58 |
| Seat Support | 1" | 13" | ³⁄₈" | 2 | Birch | Page 58 |
| Seat | 1½" | 14" | ³⁄₈" | 2 | Birch | |
| Top | ³⁄₄" | 14" | ³⁄₈" | 8 | Birch | |
| End Assembly, Reference View | | | | | | Page 59 |

# Construction Sequence: Picnic Table

1. Cut all the pieces to the sizes specified on the drawings.
2. Align the eight Top pieces. Measure and mark a line inset ¾" from each end. This line represents the location where the Top Supports attach to the Top pieces.
3. Glue and clamp the Top pieces to the Top Supports. Ensure that the Tabletop Assembly is square.
4. Align the Seat boards. Measure and mark a line inset 3/4" from each end. This line represents the location where the Seat Supports will attach to the Seats.
5. Glue and clamp the two Seat Supports to the Seat pieces. Ensure that the Seat Assembly is square.
6. Glue and clamp the Legs to the Tabletop and Seat Assemblies, following the dimensions on the End Assembly Reference drawing.
7. Glue and clamp the Angle Braces between the Seat Supports and the Tabletop Assembly.
8. Sand the table and apply a stain and a finish.

TABLES

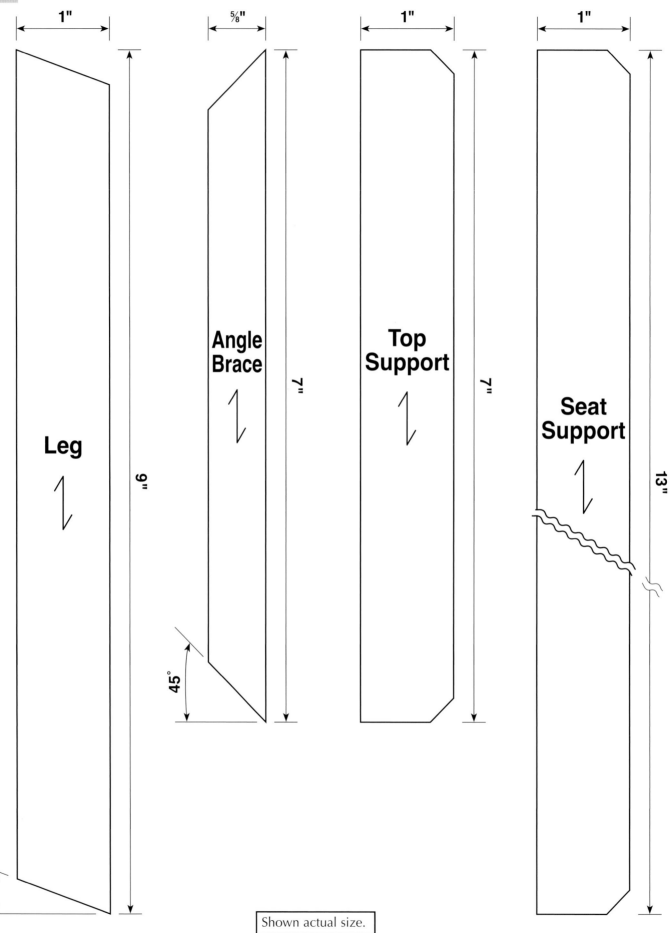

1"

⅝"

1"

1"

**Leg**

**Angle
Brace**

**Top
Support**

**Seat
Support**

9"

7"

7"

13"

45°

20°

Shown actual size.

# End Assembly

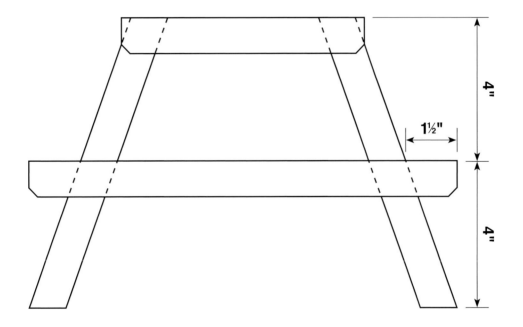

# *Southwestern-Style* Nightstand

## Materials List

| Item | Width | Length | Thickness | Quantity | Wood Type | Location |
|------|-------|--------|-----------|----------|-----------|----------|
| Top | 4" | 4½" | ⅜" | 1 | Birch | |
| Front Stretcher | ½" | 3½" | ⅜" | 2 | Cherry | Page 62 |
| End Stretcher | ½" | 2¾" | ⅜" | 2 | Cherry | Page 62 |
| End Insert | 2¾" | 3" | ¼" | 2 | Birch | Page 62 |
| Leg | ½" | 4" | ½" | 4 | Cherry | Page 62 |

# Construction Sequence: Southwestern-Style Nightstand

1. Select wood materials of the proper thickness for each part. Select wood with fine grain lines in scale with the furniture being built.
2. Lay out and cut all the pieces to the sizes specified on the drawings.

### Technical Note:

The Top will look more authentic if it is made from four 1"-wide pieces of wood glued together to form the 4"-wide Top.

3. Lay out the location and cut ⅜" deep mortises in each Leg as specified on the drawing.
4. Lay out and cut tenons on both ends of the Front Stretchers as specified on the drawing.
5. Dry fit the tenons and mortises.
6. Photocopy the pattern for the Front Stretchers. Use temporary adhesive to attach the photocopy to the board. Cut out the decorative diamond on these pieces.
7. Photocopy the pattern for the End Inserts. Use temporary adhesive to attach the photocopy to the board. Cut out the two End Inserts.
8. Cut the two End Stretchers to the width specified on the drawing and slightly longer than the length indicated on the drawing.
9. Glue and clamp the End Stretcher to the bottom end of the End Insert. Ensure that these are flush with the back surface and centered on the width of the End Insert. After the glue has dried, trim the End Stretcher flush with the End Insert.

10. Glue and clamp the End Insert between two of the Legs. Align this flush with the top of the Legs and flush with the inside edge of the Legs. Ensure that the mortises on both Legs are facing to the inside.
11. Glue and clamp the Front Stretchers and the Back Stretchers between the Leg Assemblies. Ensure that the assembly is square.
12. Glue and clamp the Top to the Leg Assembly.
13. Sand the table and apply a finish.

TABLES

Shown actual size.

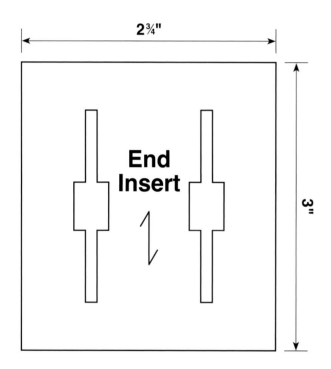

**End Insert**

2¾"

3"

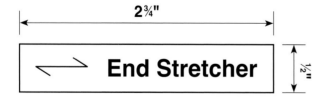

2¾"

**End Stretcher**

½"

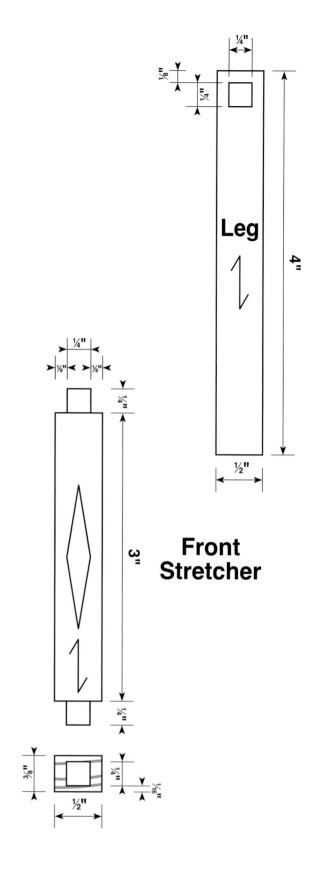

**Leg**

¼"

⅛"

¼"

4"

½"

**Front Stretcher**

¼"

⅛"

⅛"

¼"

3"

¼"

⅜"

½"

¼"

1⁄16"

# Part Four

# Doll Beds

**Page 64**

**Page 72**

**Page 77**

N ow that I've introduced the idea of a bedroom suit in the previous chapter with the plans for a Southwestern-style nightstand, let's focus on making types of beds for dolls. Here in this section, you will find projects for four beds: a canopy bed, a bunk bed, a Southwestern-style bed and a classic bed. These beds can be matched up with a variety of furniture in this book to create beautiful bedrooms that are equally suited to display or play.

When creating beds make a tight joint between the head, the footboards and the side rails. This is the critical area with the highest stress. A square should be used at assembly to help ensure that the side rails are square with the head and footboards. Personalize these beds by choosing paint colors and blanket fabrics that match the owner's bed.

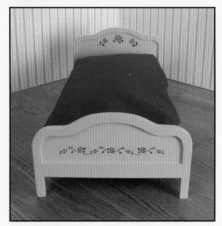

**Page 83**

# *Canopy Bed*

## Materials List

| Item | Width | Length | Thickness | Quantity | Wood Type | Location |
|------|-------|--------|-----------|----------|-----------|----------|
| End Top | 2" | 11" | ½" | 2 | Walnut | Page 69 |
| End Bottom | 1¼" | 11" | ½" | 2 | Walnut | Page 69 |
| Canopy End | 1¼" | 11" | ½" | 2 | Walnut | Page 67 |
| Canopy Side | 4⅝" | 22" | ½" | 2 | Walnut | Page 68 |
| Side Rail | 1¼" | 21½" | ½" | 2 | Walnut | Page 67 |
| Head Insert Panel | 4½" | 10½" | ¼" | 1 | Walnut | |
| Foot Insert Panel | 2¾" | 10½" | ¼" | 1 | Walnut | |
| Mattress Support | 10⅞" | 21½" | ¼" | 1 | Plywood | |
| Head Post Left | ⅝" | 16½" | ⅝" | 1 | Walnut | Page 71 |
| Head Post Right | ⅝" | 16½" | ⅝" | 1 | Walnut | Page 71 |
| Foot Post Left | ⅝" | 16½" | ⅝" | 1 | Walnut | Page 70 |
| Foot Post Right | ⅝" | 16½" | ⅝" | 1 | Walnut | Page 70 |
| Dowel Rods | ¼" | 11" | ¼" | 3 | Walnut Dowel | |

# Construction Sequence: Canopy Bed

## Making the Bed End Assembly

1. Select hardwood materials of the proper thickness for each bed part on the materials list.
2. Cut ¼" x ¼" dado grooves on the edges of the End Top and the End Bottom boards, as marked on the drawing.

### Technical Note:

The End Top and the End Bottom pieces are too small to handle safely when cutting the dados. To make this operation safer, use a 4"-wide by 22"-long board. Cut the dado on the entire length of the board before cutting the pieces to their final widths and lengths. This improves the safety of the dado operation.

3. Cut the End Top, the End Bottom and the Canopy End pieces to the widths and lengths specified on the drawings.
4. Lay out and cut the tenons on both ends of these pieces to the dimensions specified on the drawings.
5. Cut the ⅝" x ⅝" Post to the length specified on the drawings.
6. Lay out the location of the mortises specified on the drawings for the Head Post Left and the Head Post Right.
7. Use a ¼" mortise drill and cut all of the mortises to ⅜" deep and to the lengths specified on the drawings.
8. Dry assemble the tenons on these pieces with the matching mortises in the Post.
9. Lay out and cut the Head Insert Panel to the size specified on the drawing.
10. Dry assemble the Head Insert Panel with the End Top and the End Bottom pieces.
11. Photocopy the patterns for the End Top and the End Bottom pieces. Use a temporary adhesive to attach the photocopies to these pieces and cut the decorative profiles. Sand the edges of these pieces. Dry assemble the Headboard Assembly.
12. Apply glue to the tenons on the Canopy End, the End Top and the End Bottom and to the mortises on the Post.
13. Assemble the Head Insert Panel with the End Top and the End Bottom pieces.
14. Insert the tenons of these pieces into the mortises in the Head Post Left and the Head Post Right. Clamp the

Headboard Assembly. Ensure that the Headboard Assembly is square.

15. Follow the same steps outlined above to make the Footboard Assembly.

## Making the Mattress Support System

16. Cut a board 3" wide and 21" long for the Side Rail pieces.
17. Cut a ¼" x ⅛" dado groove in both edges of this board.
18. Cut the two Side Rail pieces to the width and length specified on the drawing.
19. Cut tenons on both ends of these pieces to the size specified on the drawing.
20. Dry assemble the Side Rail tenons to the mortises in the Head Post Left, the Foot Post Left, the Head Post Right and the Foot Post Right. Adjust the tenon dimensions by using a file, if needed.
21. Cut the Mattress Support to the dimensions specified on the materials list.
22. Dry assemble the Mattress Support System to the Headboard and Footboard Assemblies. **Do not glue any of these pieces yet.**
23. Select a piece of wood with clear, straight grain to be used for the Canopy Sides.
24. The board should be at least 4⅝" wide and have one straight edge.
25. Cut the board to 22" long, with both ends square to the straight edge.
26. Cut the tenons on both ends of both pieces to the dimensions specified on the drawings.
27. Photocopy the patterns for the Canopy Sides (left and right). Match up the patterns to create the entire Canopy Side pattern and ensure that the pattern is the correct length of 22". Use temporary adhesive to attach the photocopy to a scrap piece of ¼" plywood to make a test pattern. Test cut the Canopy Sides, following the photocopied lines.
28. Dry assemble the test pattern with the all other pieces of the Bed Assembly. If the test pattern does not provide a satisfactory fit, adjust the pattern as needed.
29. Drill small holes in the test pattern where the Dowel Rods will be located.
30. Lay out the Canopy Sides using the test pattern. Mark the location for the Dowel Rods.
31. Drill three ¼"-diameter holes ¼" deep at the marked locations for the Dowel Rods.
32. Cut out the Canopy Sides from walnut.
33. Smooth out the profile edges on the Canopy Sides using a spindle sander.
34. Cut three ¼"-diameter Dowel Rods to the length specified on the materials list.
35. Dry assemble the Canopy Sides with the Dowel Rods to all other pieces of the Bed Assembly.

## Assembling the Canopy Sides and the Mattress Support System

36. Apply glue to the tenons on the Side Rails, the Canopy Sides and the mortises in the Head Posts and the Foot Posts.
37. Apply glue to the dado grooves in the Side Rails and assemble the Mattress Support into the Side Rails.
38. Insert the Dowel Rods between the Canopy Sides.
39. Insert the tenons of all these pieces into the mortises in the Head Posts and the Foot Posts.
40. Ensure that the Bed Assembly is square.
41. Clamp the assembly until the glue is dry.

## Finishing

42. Sand the bed and apply a stain and a finish.

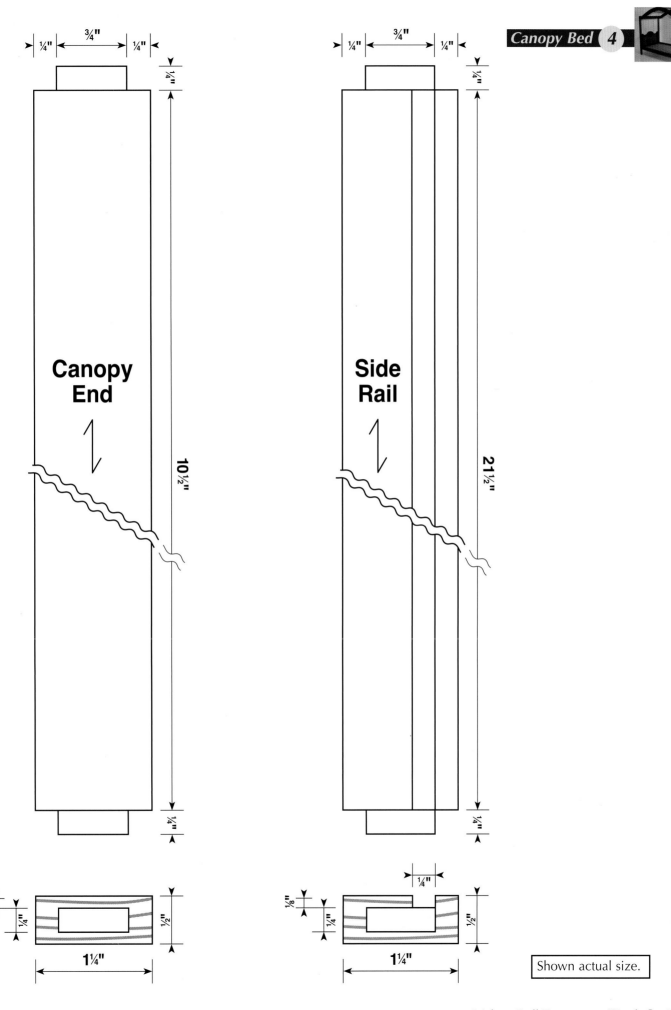

¾"

¼"   ¼"

¼"

**Canopy
End**

10½"

¼"

⅛"

¼"

½"

1¼"

¾"

¼"   ¼"

¼"

**Side
Rail**

21½"

¼"

¼"

⅛"

¼"

½"

1¼"

Shown actual size.

BEDS

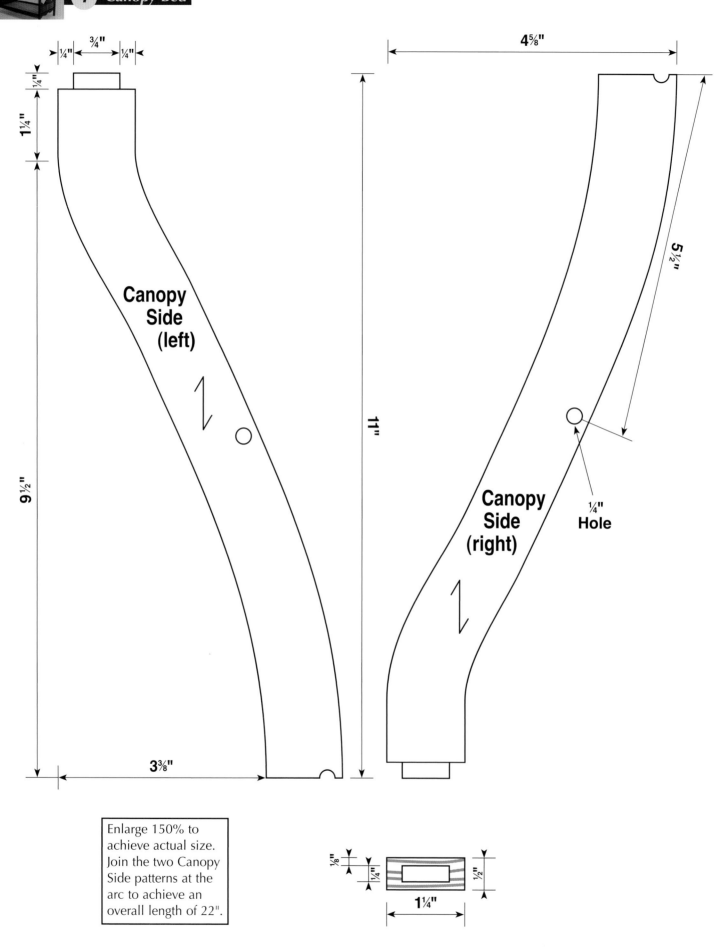

¾"
¼" ¼"
¼"
1¼"

Canopy
Side
(left)

9½"

3⅜"

11"

4⅝"

5½"

Canopy
Side
(right)

¼"
Hole

Enlarge 150% to
achieve actual size.
Join the two Canopy
Side patterns at the
arc to achieve an
overall length of 22".

⅛"
¼"
½"
1¼"

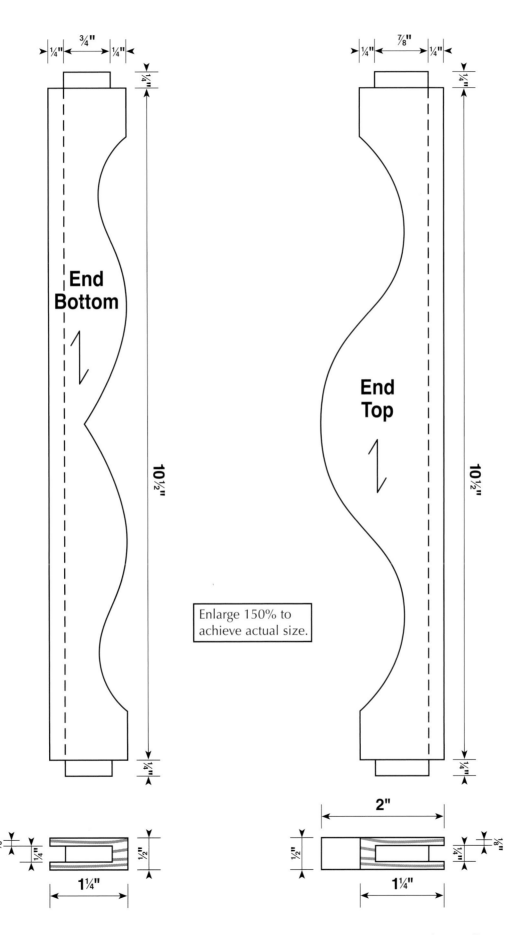

3/4"
1/4" 1/4"
1/4"

**End
Bottom**

10 1/2"

1/4"

7/8"
1/4" 1/4"
1/4"

**End
Top**

10 1/2"

1/4"

Enlarge 150% to
achieve actual size.

1/8"
1/4"
1/2"
1 1/4"

2"

1/2"
1/8"
1/4"
1 1/4"

Shown actual size.

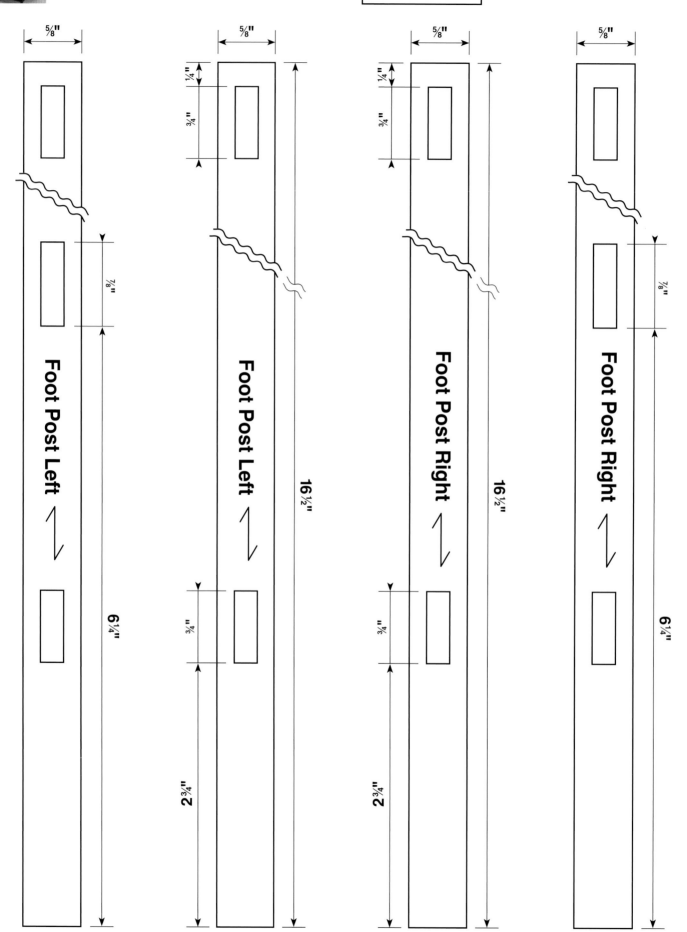

5/8"

3/4"
1/4"

7/8"

**Foot Post Left** →

6 1/4"

5/8"

3/4"
1/4"

16 1/2"

**Foot Post Left** →

3/4"

2 3/4"

5/8"

3/4"
1/4"

16 1/2"

**Foot Post Right** →

3/4"

2 3/4"

5/8"

7/8"

**Foot Post Right** →

6 1/4"

Shown actual size.

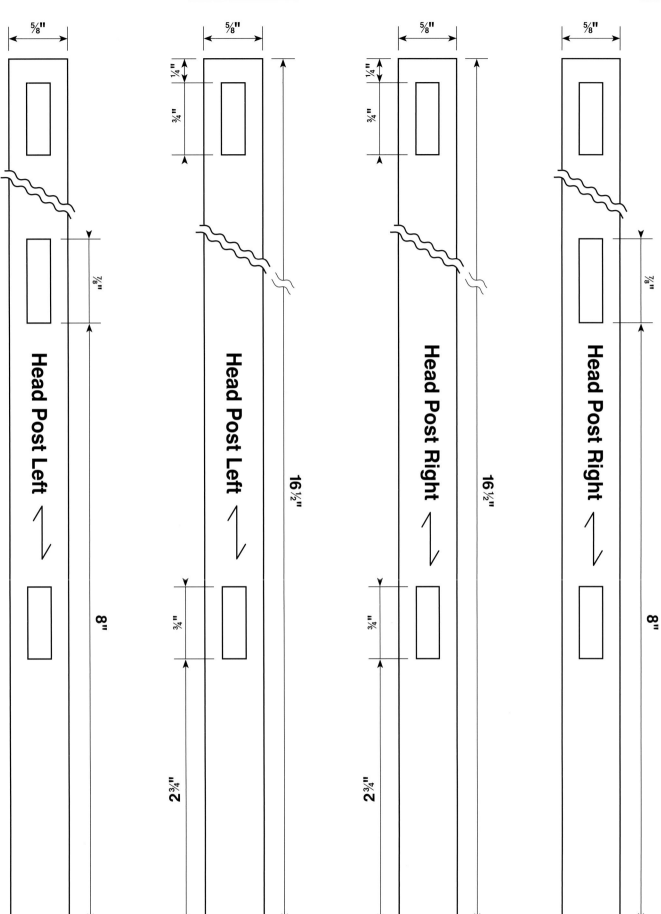

⁵⁄₈"

Head Post Left ⟶

⁷⁄₈"

8"

⁵⁄₈"

¼"
¾"

Head Post Left ⟶

16½"

¾"

2¾"

⁵⁄₈"

¼"
¾"

Head Post Right ⟶

16½"

¾"

2¾"

⁵⁄₈"

Head Post Right ⟶

⁷⁄₈"

8"

BEDS

# *Bunk Bed*

## Materials List

| Item | Width | Length | Thickness | Quantity | Wood Type | Location |
|---|---|---|---|---|---|---|
| Side Rail | 1¼" | 21½" | ½" | 2 | Hardwood | Page 76 |
| Post Left | ¾" | 21¾" | ¾" | 2 | Hardwood | Page 75 |
| Post Right | ¾" | 21¾" | ¾" | 2 | Hardwood | Page 75 |
| Top End Rail | ¾" | 10½" | ½" | 4 | Hardwood | Page 76 |
| Bottom End Rail | 1¼" | 10½" | ½" | 4 | Hardwood | Page 76 |
| End Panel | 4¾" | 10" | ¼" | 4 | Plywood | |
| Mattress Support | 10¾" | 21½" | ¼" | 1 | Plywood | |

# Construction Sequence: Bunk Bed

## Making the Bed End Assembly

1. Select hardwood materials of the proper thickness for each bed part.
2. Cut two pieces of ½"-thick wood, 2" wide and 21" long.
3. Cut dado grooves on the edge of these boards as specified on the drawings for the Top End Rails and the Bottom End Rails.
4. Using the board above, cut the End Rail pieces to the widths and lengths specified on the drawings.
5. Cut tenons on each end of the End Rail pieces as specified on the drawing.
6. Cut four Posts to the specified sizes.
7. Lay out the locations of the mortises as specified on the drawings for the Post Left and the Post Right.
8. Using a ¼" mortise drill, cut all of the mortises ⅜" deep.
9. Dry assemble the End Rail tenons with the mortises in the Posts.
10. Cut the four End Panels from ¼" plywood.
11. Apply glue to the End Rail tenons and to the Post Left and the Post Right mortises.
12. Clamp two of the End Panels with one Left Post and one Right Post. Ensure that the Bed End Assembly is square.
13. Repeat the steps outlined above for the second Bed End Assembly.

## Making the Mattress Support System

14. Cut a board 2½" wide and 21½" long for the Side Rails.
15. Cut ¼" x ¼" dado grooves on both edges of this board.
16. Cut the Side Rails from this board to the width and length specified on drawing.
17. Cut tenons on each end of the Side Rails as specified on the drawing.
18. Cut the Mattress Support to size as specified on the materials list.
19. Dry assemble the Side Rail tenons to the mortises in the Bed End Assemblies.

## Assembling the Bed End Assemblies to the Side Rails

20. Apply glue to the tenons on the Side Rails and to the mortises in the Bed End Assemblies.
21. Apply glue to the dado grooves in the Side Rails and assemble the Mattress Support with the Side Rails.
22. Insert the tenons of the Side Rails into the mortises on the Bed End Assemblies.
23. Assemble both upper and lower Mattress Support Assemblies with both Bed End Assemblies.
24. Ensure that the assembly is square.
25. Clamp the assembled bed until the glue is dry.

**BEDS**

## Finishing

26. Sand the bed and apply a finish.

27. Apply stencils (available at hobby and craft stores in miniature sizes) as desired.

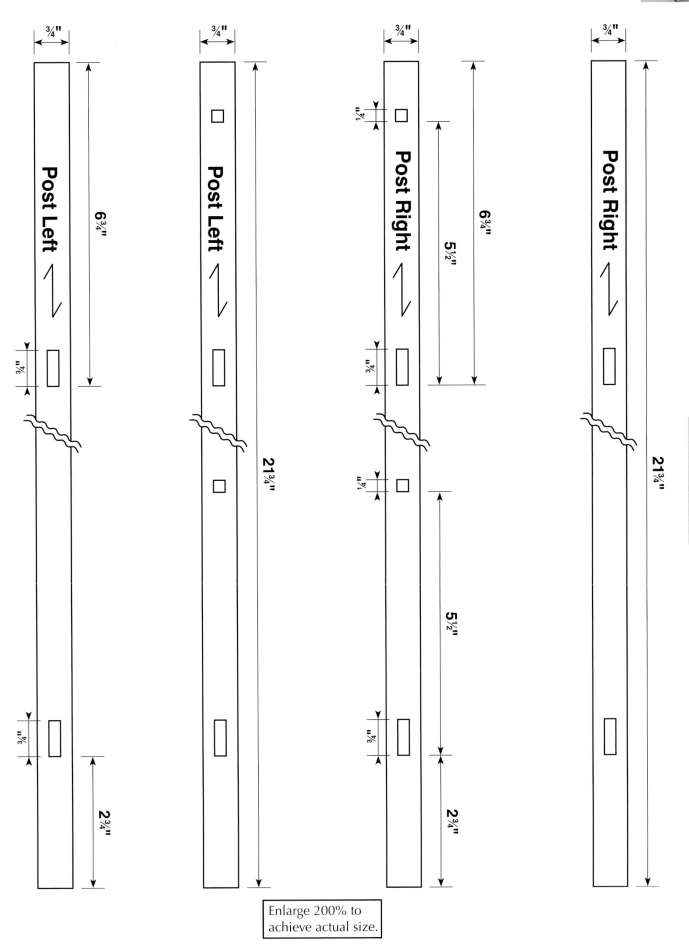

¾"

Post Left →

6¾"

¾"

2¾"

¾"

Post Left →

21¾"

¾"

¼"

Post Right →

6¾"

5½"

¼"

3¾"

5½"

2¾"

¾"

Post Right →

21¾"

Enlarge 200% to achieve actual size.

BEDS

Making Doll Furniture in Wood ○ 75

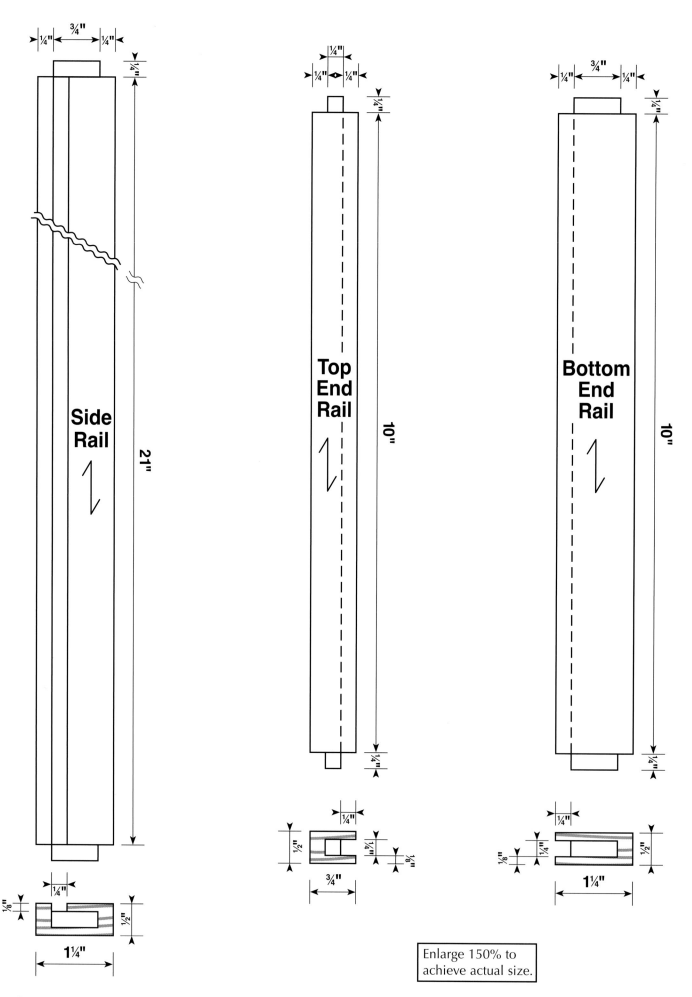

¾"
¼"  ¼"
¼"

**Side Rail**

21"

⅛"
¼"
½"
1¼"

¼"
¼"  ¼"
¼"

**Top End Rail**

10"

¼"

½"
¼"
⅛"
¼"
¾"

¾"
¼"  ¼"
¼"

**Bottom End Rail**

10"

¼"

⅛"
¼"
½"
¼"
1¼"

Enlarge 150% to achieve actual size.

# Southwestern-Style
# Bed

## Materials List

| Item | Width | Length | Thickness | Quantity | Wood Type | Location |
|---|---|---|---|---|---|---|
| Long Post | ½" | 7" | ½" | 2 | Cherry | Page 82 |
| Short Post | ½" | 5¼" | ½" | 2 | Cherry | Page 82 |
| Side Rail | 1¼" | 21" | ½" | 2 | Poplar | Page 82 |
| Headboard | 6½" | 10½" | ⅜" | 1 | Poplar | Page 81 |
| Footboard | 4⅜" | 10½" | ⅜" | 1 | Poplar | Page 80 |
| Mattress Support | 11" | 21" | ¼" | 1 | Plywood | |

# Construction Sequence: Southwestern-Style Bed

## Making the Bed End Assembly

1. Select hardwood materials of the proper thickness for each bed part on the materials list.
2. Cut the Long Post to the dimensions specified on drawing.
3. Lay out the locations of the mortises as specified on the drawing for the Long Post.
4. Using a ¼" mortise drill and mortise attachment, drill all mortises ⅜" deep.
5. Photocopy the pattern for the Headboard. Using temporary adhesive, attach the copy to the ⅜"-thick wood selected for the Headboard.
6. Drill pilot holes on the Headboard for all the inside cuts to prepare the piece for scroll sawing.
7. Cut out the Headboard using a scroll saw.
8. Ensure that the end cuts on the length of the Headboard are straight and square.
9. Measure and mark the Long Post 1¼" from the bottom. This is the location where the Headboard will attach to the Long Post.
10. Apply glue to the ends of the Headboard and clamp it to the Long Post. Ensure that the ⅜"-thick Headboard is centered on the ½" thickness of the Long Post and aligned with the marks. Ensure that the mortises are both located on the same side of the Headboard Assembly.
11. Follow the same steps outlined above to make the Footboard Assembly.

## Making the Mattress Support System

12. Cut a board 3" wide and 21" long for the Side Rail pieces.
13. Cut a ¼" x ⅛" dado groove on both edges of this board.
14. From the 3" board, cut the Side Rail pieces to the width and length specified on drawing.
15. Cut the tenons on each end of the Side Rails to the size specified on the drawing.
16. From ¼" plywood, cut the Mattress Support to the dimensions specified on the materials list.
17. Dry assemble the Side Rails and the Mattress Support to the Post. (Adjust the tenon dimensions with a file if needed.)

## Assembling the Headboard and Footboard Assemblies to the Side Rails

18. Apply glue to the tenons on each Side Rail and to the mortises in the Long Posts.
19. Apply glue in the dado grooves in the Side Rails.
20. Assemble the Mattress Support with the Side Rails.
21. Insert the Side Rail tenons into the mortises on the Long Posts of the Headboard Assembly. Clamp the assembly until the glue is dry.
22. Ensure that the assembly is square.

23. Follow the same steps outlined above to assemble the Footboard to the Side Rails.

## Finishing
24. Sand the bed and apply a finish.

4⅜"

10½"

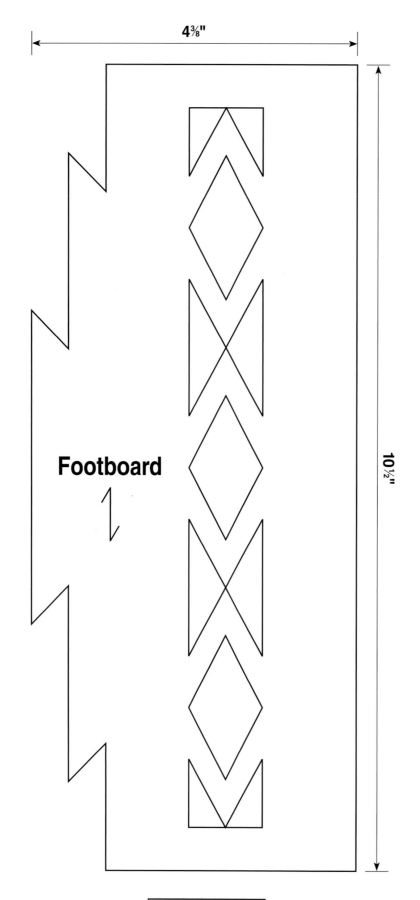

**Footboard**

Enlarge 125% to achieve actual size.

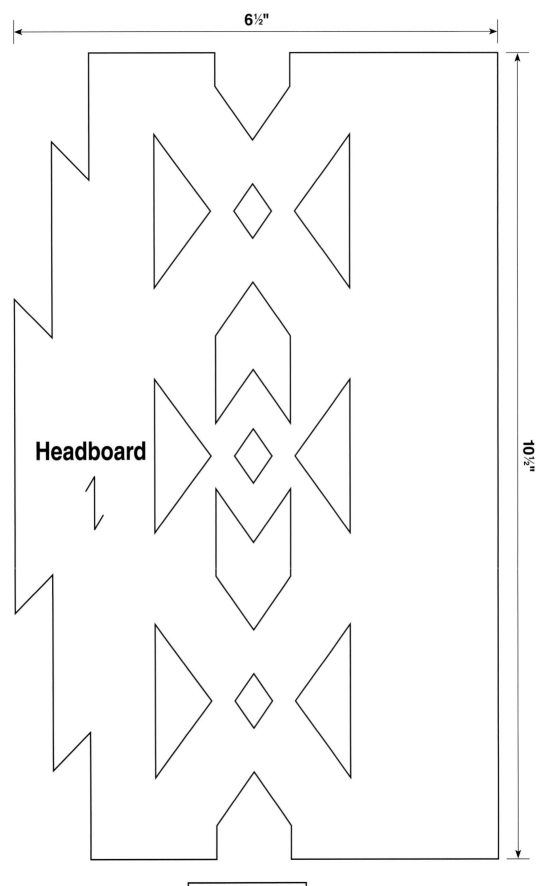

6½"

**Headboard**

10½"

Enlarge 125% to
achieve actual size.

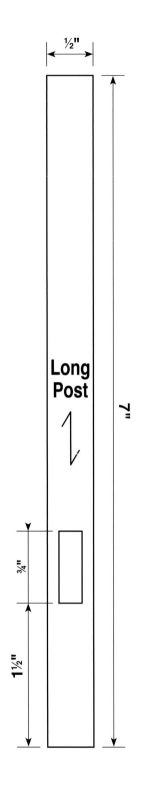

½"

**Long
Post**

7"

¾"

1½"

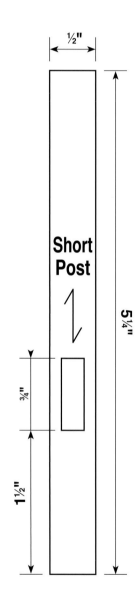

½"

**Short
Post**

5¼"

¾"

1½"

Shown actual size.

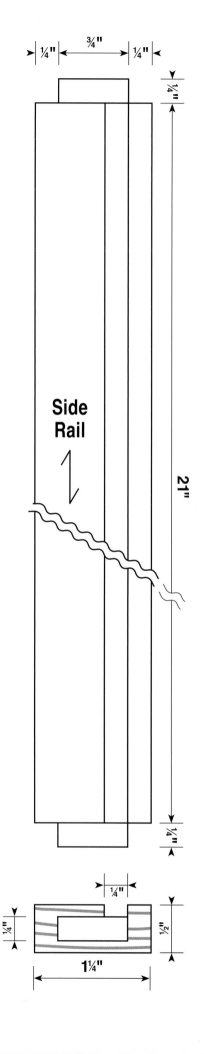

¼"   ¾"   ¼"

¼"

**Side
Rail**

21"

¼"

¼"

¼"

½"

1¼"

# Classic Bed

## Materials List

| Item | Width | Length | Thickness | Quantity | Wood Type | Location |
|---|---|---|---|---|---|---|
| Top (Head & Foot) | 3" | 11½" | ½" | 2 | Poplar | Page 87 |
| Head Panel | 5⅛" | 10¼" | ¼" | 1 | Poplar | Page 88 |
| Foot Panel | 3¼" | 10¼" | ¼" | 1 | Poplar | Page 88 |
| Stretcher | 1¼" | 10¼" | ½" | 2 | Poplar | |
| Head Leg | ⅝" | 6" | ½" | 2 | Poplar | |
| Foot Leg | ⅝" | 4" | ½" | 2 | Poplar | |
| Side Rail | 1¼" | 21" | ½" | 2 | Poplar | Page 86 |
| End Rail | 1¼" | 10½" | ½" | 2 | Poplar | Page 86 |
| Mattress Support | 11" | 20½" | ¼" | 1 | Plywood | |

# Construction Sequence: Classic Bed

## Making the Mattress Support System

1. Select wood materials of the proper thickness for each bed part on the materials list.
2. Cut two boards to a width of 2½" and a length of 21" to be used for the Side Rail and the End Rail pieces.
3. Cut ¼" x ¼" dado grooves on both edges of these boards as specified on the drawings.
4. Cut the Side Rail and the End Rail pieces to the widths and lengths specified on drawings.
5. Cut the Mattress Support to the size specified on the materials list.
6. Dry fit the Mattress Support, the End Rails and the Side Rails. The End Rails fit between the Side Rails and are flush with the ends of the Side Rails.
7. Apply glue to the ends of the End Rails and in the dado groove of the Side Rails.
8. Glue and clamp the assembly and the Mattress Support.
9. Ensure that the End Rail pieces are flush and square with the ends of the Side Rails.

## Making the Headboard and Footboard Assemblies

10. Photocopy the two patterns for the Top (Head & Foot) pieces. Use temporary adhesive to attach the photocopies to the wood selected for these parts.
11. Cut the two Top pieces, following the lines on the photocopied pattern.
12. Sand the edges of these pieces to remove any imperfections in the cutting.
13. Photocopy the pattern for the Head Panel. Use temporary adhesive to attach the photocopy to the wood selected for the Head Panel.
14. Use the Top piece (cut in the previous steps) to check the fit of the inside of the Top piece and the corresponding curved sections on the paper pattern. Re-mark the paper pattern, if necessary.
15. Cut out the Head Panel by carefully following the lines on the photocopied pattern.
16. Glue and clamp the Top piece to the Head Panel. Ensure that the Top piece is flush with one face of the Head Panel.
17. Cut the Stretcher to the dimensions specified on the drawing.

Ensure that the length of the Stretcher specified on the drawing matches the length of the Head Panel made above. If the cut result is different than that specified on the drawing, adjust the length as necessary.

18. Glue and clamp the Stretcher to the bottom of the Head Panel. Ensure that the Stretcher is flush with the face of the Head Panel.
19. Cut the Head Legs to the size specified on the drawing.
20. Glue and clamp the Head Legs to each side of the Headboard Assembly.
21. Follow the same steps outlined above to make the Footboard Assembly.

## Assembling the bed

22. Dry assemble the Headboard Assembly to the Mattress Support.
23. Check to ensure that the Headboard Assembly is square when it is clamped to the Mattress Support System. If it is not square, adjust the fit of the Side Rails using a disc sander.
24. Glue and clamp the Headboard Assembly to the Mattress Support System.
25. Ensure that the bottoms of the Side. Rails align with the bottom of the Stretcher on the Headboard Assembly.
26. Follow the same steps outlined above to attach the Footboard Assembly to the Mattress Support.

## Finishing

27. Sand the bed and apply a finish.
28. Stencils in miniature sizes are available at hobby and craft stores.

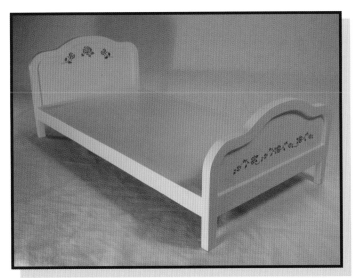

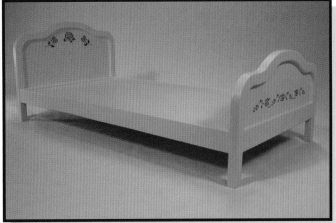

BEDS

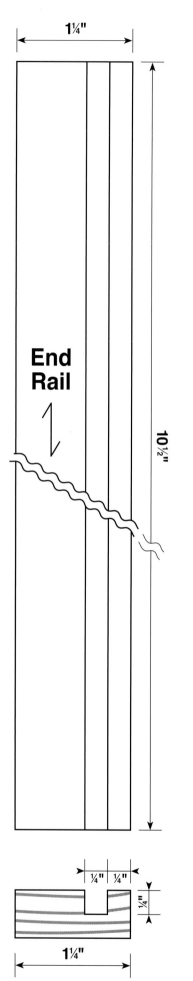

1¼"

**End Rail**

10½"

¼" ¼"

¼"

1¼"

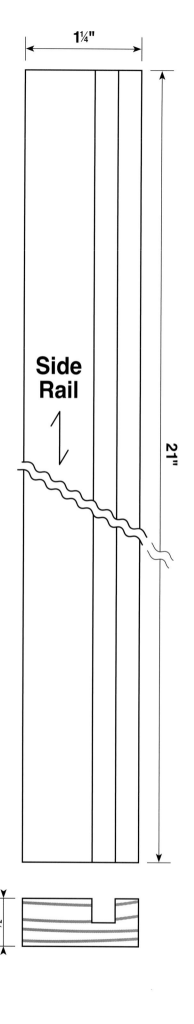

1¼"

**Side Rail**

21"

½"

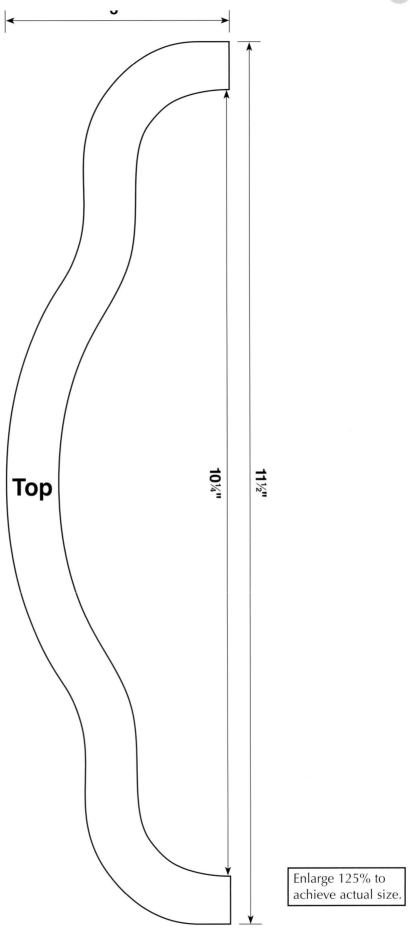

**Top**

10¼"

11½"

Enlarge 125% to
achieve actual size.

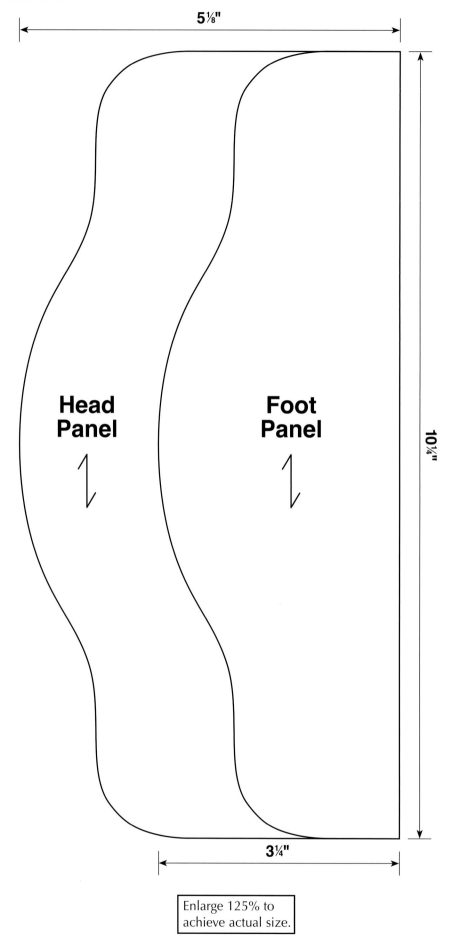

5⅛"

**Head Panel**

**Foot Panel**

10¼"

3¼"

Enlarge 125% to
achieve actual size.

Part Five

# Dressers & Chests

*Page 90*

*Page 99*

W hat bedroom suit would be complete without a dresser or chest in which to store the many clothes and accessories dolls seems to accumulate. Here in this chapter you will find plans for four dressers and chests: a tall chest, a short chest, an armoire and a treasure chest.

Essentially chests are boxes with simple glue joints. The important focus is to make the drawers square and sized to operate smoothly. The drawers are made with plywood except for the fronts. The chest tops and armoire panels could be made by gluing narrow boards together to create a look more authentic and to scale for doll size furniture.

*Page 107*

*Page 116*

# Tall Chest

## Materials List

| Item | Width | Length | Thickness | Quantity | Wood Type | Location |
|---|---|---|---|---|---|---|
| Left Leg | 1½" | 11" | ½" | 1 | Walnut | Page 96 |
| Right Leg | 1½" | 11" | ½" | 1 | Walnut | Page 96 |
| Back Leg | ½" | 11" | ½" | 2 | Walnut | Page 95 |
| Insert Panel | 4¼" | 10" | ¼" | 2 | Walnut | |
| Side Rail | ⅝" | 4 ¼" | ⅜" | 2 | Walnut | Page 98 |
| Back | 10¼" | 10½" | ¼" | 1 | Walnut | |
| Drawer Support Panel | 4¼" | 9¾" | ¼" | 5 | Walnut | Page 98 |
| Support Stretcher | ⅝" | 10¼" | ⅜" | 4 | Walnut | Page 98 |
| Bottom Stretcher | 1" | 10¼" | ⅜" | 1 | Walnut | Page 94 |
| Chest Top | 6" | 11¼" | ⅜" | 1 | Walnut | |
| Drawer Front #1 | 1¼" | 9¾" | ⅜" | 1 | Walnut | Page 95 |
| Drawer Front #2 | 1¾" | 9¾" | ⅜" | 1 | Walnut | Page 95 |
| Drawer Front #3 | 2½" | 9¾" | ⅜" | 1 | Walnut | Page 95 |
| Drawer Front #4 | 3" | 9¾" | ⅜" | 1 | Walnut | Page 95 |
| Drawer Side #1 | 1" | 4¾" | ¼" | 2 | Plywood | Page 97 |
| Drawer Side #2 | 1½" | 4¾" | ¼" | 2 | Plywood | Page 97 |
| Drawer Side #3 | 2¼" | 4¾" | ¼" | 2 | Plywood | Page 97 |
| Drawer Side #4 | 2¾" | 4¾" | ¼" | 2 | Plywood | Page 97 |
| Drawer Back #1 | 1" | 9¼" | ¼" | 1 | Plywood | Page 97 |
| Drawer Back #2 | 1½" | 9¼" | ¼" | 1 | Plywood | Page 97 |
| Drawer Back #3 | 2¼" | 9¼" | ¼" | 1 | Plywood | Page 97 |
| Drawer Back #4 | 2¾" | 9¼" | ¼" | 1 | Plywood | Page 97 |
| Drawer Bottom | 4¾" | 9¾" | ¼" | 4 | Plywood | |
| Side Panel Assembly | | | | | | Page 94 |
| Wood Knobs | | | ⅝" Dia. | 8 | | |

## Construction Sequence: Tall Chest

### Making the Side Panel Assemblies

1. Select hardwood materials of the proper thickness for each chest part.
2. Cut the material to the sizes specified on the drawings for the Left Leg and the Right Leg.
3. Photocopy the drawings for these Legs. Use temporary adhesive to attach the photocopy to the wood.
4. Lay out the locations of the mortises as specified on the drawings for the Left Leg and the Right Leg.
5. Use a ¼" mortise drill to cut all mortises to ⅜" deep and to the lengths specified on the drawings. Do not cut the decorative shape on the front edge of these Legs at this time.
6. Cut a ½"-thick board to 11" long and an oversized width. This board will be used to make the Back Legs.

### Technical Note:

The Back Legs have a rabbet cut on the edge. The finished size of these pieces is ½" x ½". These finished pieces would be too small to handle safely when cutting the rabbet. Using a board of an oversized width improves the safety of this operation.

DRESSERS/CHESTS

7. Cut a rabbet on both edges (on the oversized-width board) as specified on the drawing for the Back Legs.
8. From the oversized board, cut the Back Leg pieces to the width specified on the drawing.
9. Cut the Insert Panel pieces to the size specified on the drawing.
10. Cut the Side Rail pieces to the size specified on the drawing.
11. Apply glue to the end of the Insert Panel and clamp it to the Side Rail. Ensure that the Side Rail is flush with the face of the Insert Panel.
12. Apply glue to the edge of the Insert Panel and clamp it to the Left Front Leg. Ensure that the Insert Panel is flush with the side of the Front Leg with mortises and flush with the top end of the Front Leg.
13. Apply glue to the edge of the Insert Panel and clamp it to the Back Leg. Ensure that the Insert Panel is flush with the inside and top of the Back Leg. Reference the Left Side Assembly drawing for proper orientation of the Back Leg.
14. Use the same procedure outlined above to assemble the Right Side Assembly.

## Making the Chest Assembly

15. Cut the Support Stretcher and the Bottom Stretcher pieces to the sizes specified on the drawings.
16. Lay out and cut the tenons on these pieces as specified on the drawings.
17. Dry fit the tenons into the mortises in the Left Side Assembly and the Right Side Assembly.
18. Photocopy the drawing for the Bottom Stretcher. Use temporary adhesive to attach the photocopied pattern to the Bottom Stretcher and cut out the decorative shape on the lower edge.
19. Cut the Drawer Support Panels to the size specified on the drawing.
20. Glue and clamp these panels to the edges of the Support Stretchers, as shown on the drawing.
21. Glue to edge of the remaining Drawer Support Panel and clamp it to the top inside edge of the Bottom Stretcher. (This forms a 90-degree angle.)
22. Dry assemble the Left Side Assembly and the Right Side Assembly with the Drawer Supports.

> **Technical Note:**
>
> Mark a pencil line on the inside of the Left Side Assembly and on the inside of the Right Side Assembly where the Drawer Supports should align. Use a square to ensure that the line is square with the Side Assemblies. This line will be used during the glue-up process to ensure that the Drawer Supports are square with the Side Panel Assemblies.

23. Cut the decorative front edges on both Front Legs. Use the lines on the photocopy as a guide. (The photocopy was attached in the first section of the construction sequence.)
24. Apply glue to the tenons, the ends of all Drawer Support Panels, and the mortises in the Front Legs. Clamp the assembly together, ensuring that all Drawer Supports are aligned with the pencil marks and square with the Side Panel Assemblies.
25. Cut the Back to the size specified on the materials list. Confirm that the width dimension specified on the materials list matches the Chest Assembly made in the previous steps. Alter it, if needed.
26. Apply glue to the rabbets in the Back Legs and along the back edge of the Drawer Supports. Clamp the Back to the Chest Assembly and make sure that it is flush with the top ends of the Back Legs.
27. Cut the Chest Top to the size specified on the materials list.
28. Apply glue to the top surface of the top Drawer Support Panel and clamp the Chest Top to the Chest Assembly. Ensure that the Chest Top is centered on the width of the Chest Assembly and flush with the Back.

## Making the Drawers

29. Cut the Drawer Fronts to the sizes specified on the materials list.
30. Cut the rabbet on each Drawer Front as specified.
31. Cut the materials for the Drawer Sides, the Drawer Backs and the Drawer Bottoms to the sizes specified on the materials list.

### Technical Note:

Dry fit each Drawer Unit and test fit the Drawers into the Chest Assembly. Adjust the Drawer pieces before assembly. Use tape to temporarily hold the Drawer pieces together.

32. Glue and clamp the Drawer Sides, the Drawer Backs and the Drawer Bottoms to the Drawer Fronts.
33. Mark the locations for the Wood Knobs and mount them. Inset the Wood Knobs 1" from each end and centered on the Drawer width.

## Finishing

34. Sand the chest and apply a finish.

DRESSERS/CHESTS

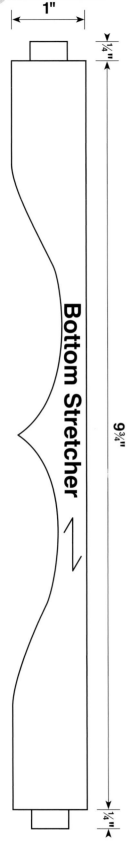

1"

¼"

Bottom Stretcher

9¾"

¼"

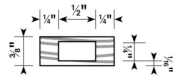

¼" ½" ¼"

⅜"

¼"

1/16"

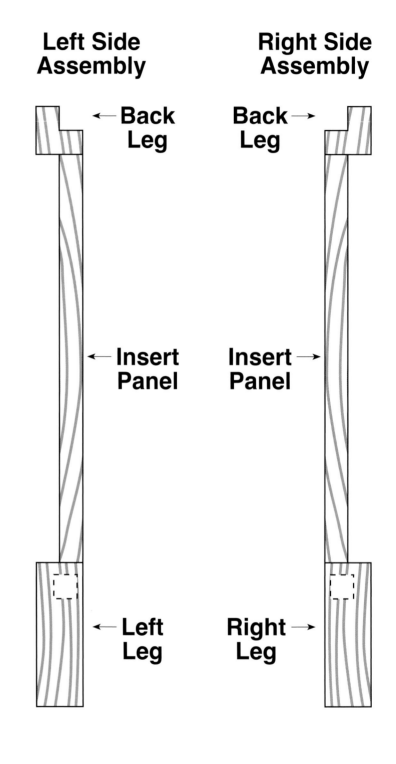

## Left Side Assembly

← **Back Leg**

← **Insert Panel**

← **Left Leg**

## Right Side Assembly

**Back Leg** →

**Insert Panel** →

**Right Leg** →

Enlarge 125% to achieve actual size.

3"     2½"     1¾"     1¼"

½"

**Drawer Front**

**Back Leg**

9¾"

11"

#4     #3     #2     #1

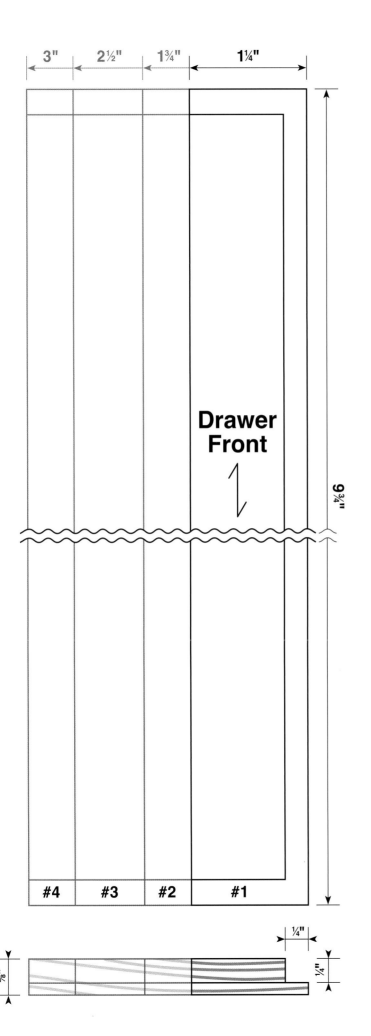

¼"

¼"

⅜"

¼"

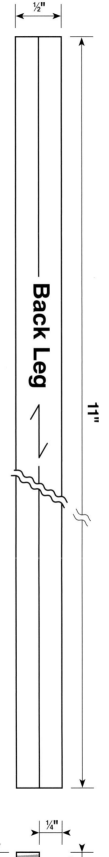

¼"

½"

¼"

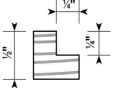

Shown actual size.

DRESSERS/CHESTS

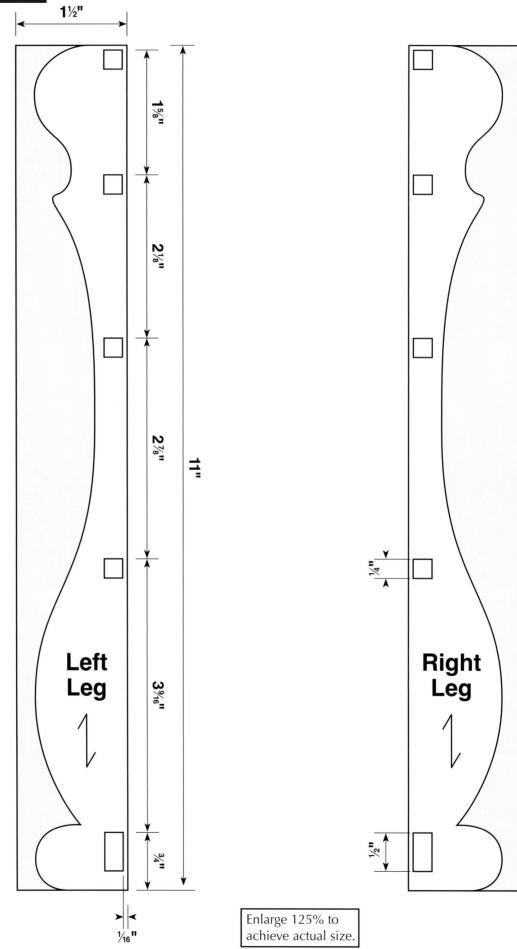

1½"

1⅝"

2⅛"

2⅞"

11"

Left
Leg

3⁹⁄₁₆"

¾"

¼"

Right
Leg

½"

¹⁄₁₆"

Enlarge 125% to
achieve actual size.

2¾"  2¼"  1½"  1"

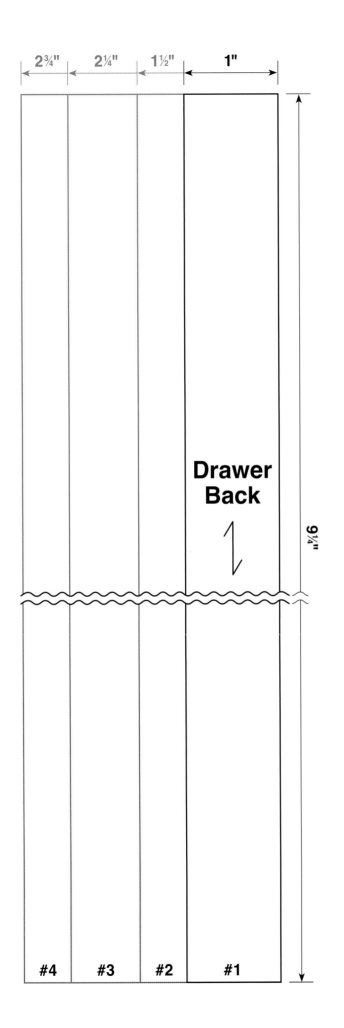

**Drawer
Back**

9¼"

#4  #3  #2  #1

2¾"  2¼"  1½"  1"

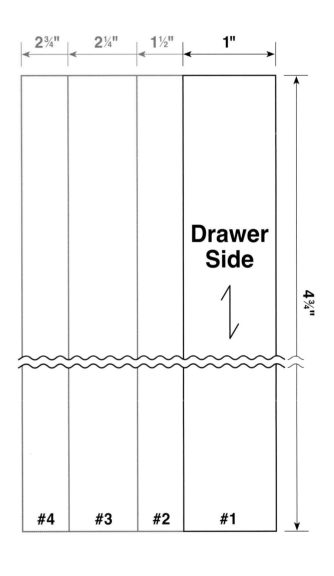

**Drawer
Side**

4¾"

#4  #3  #2  #1

Shown actual size.

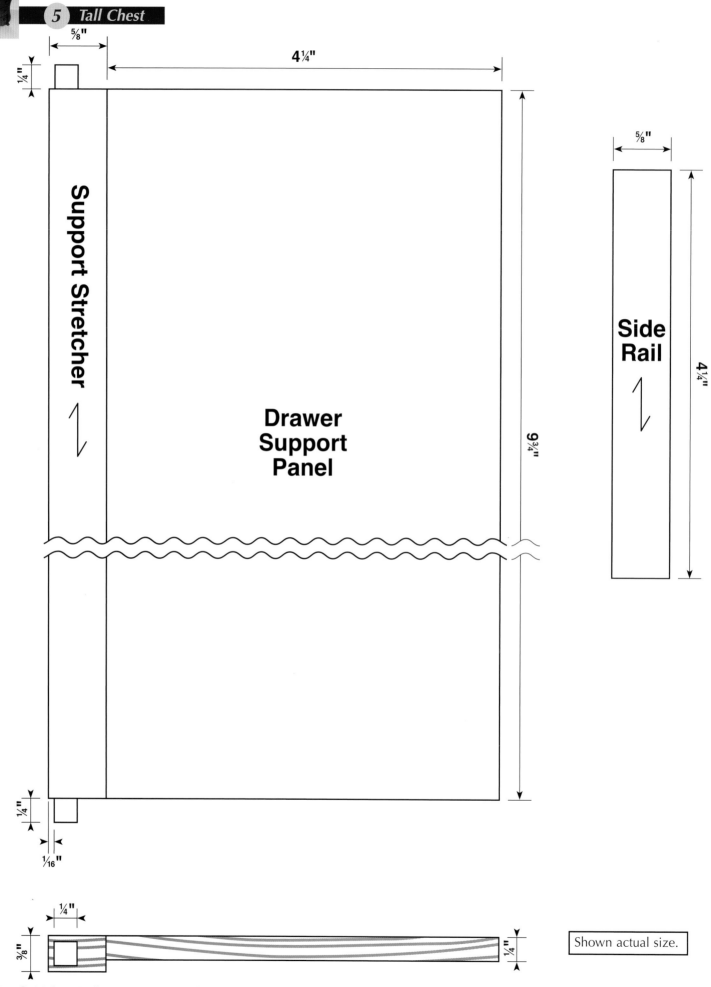

⅝"

4¼"

¼"

Support Stretcher

Drawer
Support
Panel

9¾"

⅝"

Side
Rail

4¼"

¼"

¼"

1⁄16 "

¼"

⅜"

¼"

Shown actual size.

# *Short Chest*

## Materials List

| Item | Width | Length | Thickness | Quantity | Wood Type | Location |
|---|---|---|---|---|---|---|
| Left Leg | 1½" | 7" | ½" | 1 | Walnut | Page 103 |
| Right Leg | 1½" | 7" | ½" | 1 | Walnut | Page 103 |
| Back Leg | ½" | 7" | ½" | 2 | Walnut | Page 104 |
| Insert Panel | 4¼" | 6" | ¼" | 2 | Walnut | Page 105 |
| Side Rail | ⅝" | 4¼" | ⅜" | 2 | Walnut | |
| Back | 6¼" | 6⅝" | ¼" | 1 | Walnut | |
| Drawer Support Panel | 4¼" | 5¾" | ¼" | 4 | Walnut | Page 104 |
| Support Stretcher | ⅝" | 6¼" | ⅜" | 3 | Walnut | Page 104 |
| Bottom Stretcher | 1" | 5¾" | ⅜" | 1 | Walnut | Page 105 |
| Chest Top | 6" | 7¼" | ⅜" | 1 | Walnut | |
| Drawer Front #1 | 1¼" | 5¾" | ⅜" | 1 | Walnut | Page 106 |
| Drawer Front #2 | 1⅝" | 5¾" | ⅜" | 1 | Walnut | Page 106 |
| Drawer Front #3 | 2" | 5¾" | ⅜" | 1 | Walnut | Page 106 |
| Drawer Side #1 | 1" | 4¾" | ¼" | 2 | Plywood | Page 106 |
| Drawer Side #2 | 1⅜" | 4¾" | ¼" | 2 | Plywood | Page 106 |
| Drawer Side #3 | 1¾" | 4¾" | ¼" | 2 | Plywood | Page 106 |
| Drawer Back #1 | 1" | 5¼" | ¼" | 1 | Plywood | Page 106 |
| Drawer Back #2 | 1⅜" | 5¼" | ¼" | 1 | Plywood | Page 106 |
| Drawer Back #3 | 1¾" | 5¼" | ¼" | 1 | Plywood | Page 106 |
| Drawer Bottom | 4¾" | 5¾" | ¼" | 3 | Plywood | |
| Left Side Assembly | | | | | | Page 105 |
| Right Side Assembly | | | | | | Page 105 |
| Wood Knob | | | ⅝" Dia. | 6 | | |

# Construction Sequence: Short Chest

## Making the Side Panel Assemblies

1. Select hardwood materials of the proper thickness for each chest part.
2. Cut the materials to the sizes specified on the drawings for the Left Leg and the Right Leg.
3. Photocopy the drawings for these Legs. Use temporary adhesive to attach the photocopy to the wood pieces.
4. Lay out the locations of the mortises as specified on the drawings for the Left Leg and the Right Leg pieces.
5. Use a ¼" mortise drill to cut all mortises ⅜" deep and to the length specified on the drawings. **Do not cut the decorative shape on the front edge of the Legs at this time.**
6. Cut a ½" board to 11" long and an oversized width. This board will be used to make the Back Legs.

> **Technical Note:**
>
> The Back Legs have a rabbet cut on the edge. The finished size of these pieces is ½" x ½". These finished sizes are too small to handle safely when cutting the rabbet. Using a board with an oversized width improves the safety of this operation.

7. Cut a rabbet on both edges of the oversized board as specified on the drawing for the Back Legs.

8. Cut the Back Leg pieces from the oversized board to the width specified on the drawing.

9. Cut the Insert Panel pieces to the size specified on the drawing.

10. Cut the Side Rail pieces to the size specified on the drawing.

11. Apply glue to the end of the Insert Panel and clamp it to the Side Rail. Ensure that the Side Rail is flush with the face of the Insert Panel.

12. Apply glue to the edge of the Insert Panel and clamp it to the Left Leg. Ensure that the Insert Panel is flush with the side of the Front Leg with mortises and flush with the top end of the Front Leg.

13. Apply glue to the edge of the Insert Panel and clamp it to the Back Leg. Ensure that the Insert Panel is flush with the inside and top of the Back Leg. Reference the Left Side Assembly drawing for proper orientation of the Back Leg.

14. Use the same procedure outlined above to assemble the Right Side Assembly.

## Making the Chest Assembly

15. Cut the Support Stretcher and Bottom Stretcher pieces to the sizes specified on the drawings.

16. Lay out and cut the tenons on these pieces as specified on the drawings.

17. Dry fit the tenons into the mortises in the Left Side Assembly and the Right Side Assembly.

18. Photocopy the drawing for the Bottom Stretcher. Use temporary adhesive to attach the photocopied pattern to the Bottom Stretcher and cut out the decorative shape on the lower edge.

19. Cut the Drawer Support Panels to the size specified on the drawing.

20. Glue and clamp the Drawer Support Panels to the edge of the Support Stretcher, as shown in the drawing.

21. Glue to edge of the remaining Drawer Support Panel and clamp it to the Top inside edge of the Bottom Stretcher. (This forms a 90-degree angle.)

22. Dry assemble the Left Side Assembly and the Right Side Assembly with the Drawer Supports.

### Technical Note:

Mark a pencil line on the inside of the Left Side Assembly and on the inside of the Right Side Assembly where the Drawer Supports should align. Use a square to ensure that the line is square with the Side Assemblies. This line will be used during the glue-up process to ensure that the Drawer Supports are square with the Side Panel Assemblies.

23. Cut the decorative front edges on both Front Legs. Use the lines on the photocopy as a guide. (The photocopy was attached in the first section of the construction sequence.)

24. Apply glue to the tenons, the ends of all Drawer Support Panels, and the mortises in the Front Legs. Clamp the assembly together, ensuring that all Drawer Supports are aligned with the pencil marks and square with the Side Panel Assemblies.

25. Cut the Back to the size specified on the materials list. Confirm that the width dimension specified on the materials list matches the Chest Assembly made in the previous steps.

26. Apply glue to the rabbets in the Back Legs and along the back edge of the Drawer Supports. Clamp the Back to the Chest Assembly and ensure that it is flush with the top ends of the Back Legs.

27. Cut the Chest Top to the size specified on the materials list.

28. Apply glue to the top surface of the top Drawer Support Panel and clamp the Chest Top to the Chest

Assembly. Ensure that the Chest Top is centered on the width of the Chest Assembly and flush with the Back.

## Making the Drawers

29. Cut the Drawer Fronts to the sizes specified on the drawings.
30. Cut the rabbet on each Drawer Front as specified on the drawings.
31. Cut the materials for the Drawer Sides, the Drawer Backs and the Drawer Bottoms to the sizes specified on the drawings and the materials list.

> ### Technical Note:
>
> Dry fit each Drawer Unit and test fit the Drawers into the Chest Assembly. Adjust the Drawer pieces before assembly. Use tape to temporarily hold the Drawer pieces together.

32. Glue and clamp the Drawer Sides, the Drawer Backs and the Drawer Bottoms to the Drawer Fronts.
33. Mark the locations of the Wood Knobs and mount them on the Drawers. Inset the Wood Knobs 1" from each end and centered on the Drawer width.

## Finishing

34. Sand the chest and apply a finish.

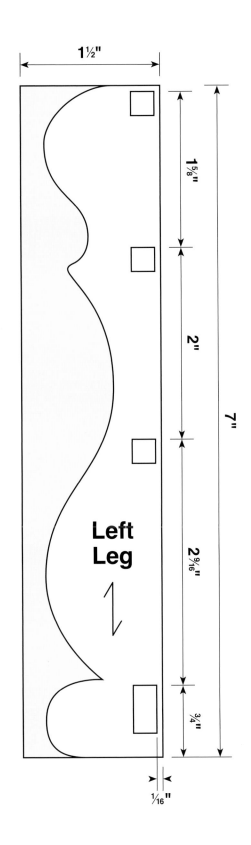

**1½"**

**1⅝"**

**2"**

**7"**

**Left
Leg**

**2⁹⁄₁₆"**

**¾"**

**¹⁄₁₆"**

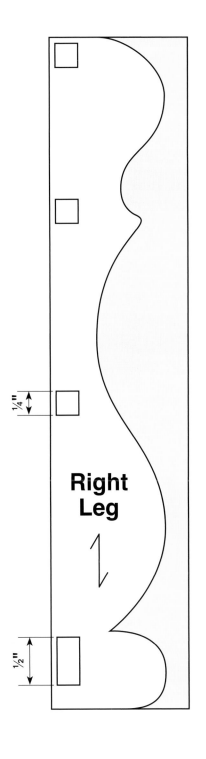

**Right
Leg**

**¼"**

**½"**

DRESSERS/CHESTS

Shown actual size.

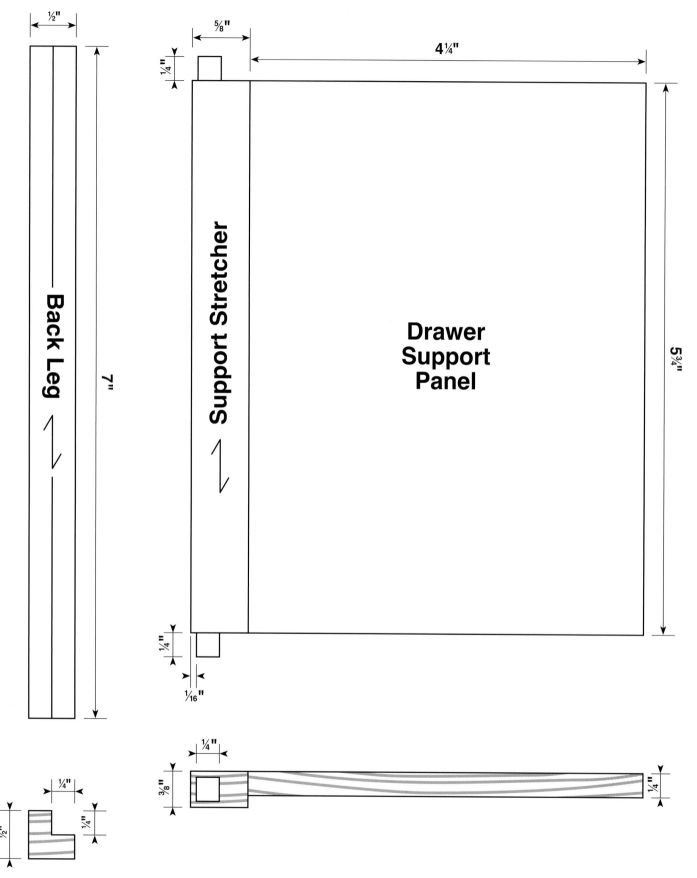

½"

⅝"

4¼"

¼"

**Back Leg**

7"

**Support Stretcher**

**Drawer
Support
Panel**

5¾"

¼"

¹⁄₁₆"

¼"

¼"

½"

¼"

¼"

⅜"

¼"

Shown actual size.

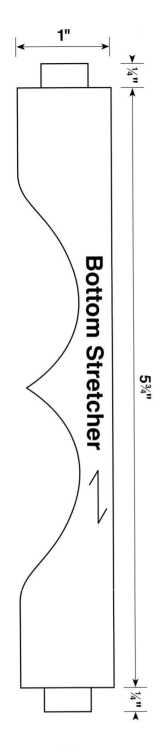

1"

¼"

5¾"

Bottom Stretcher

¼"

¼" ½" ¼"

3⁄8"

¼"

1⁄16"

Shown actual size.

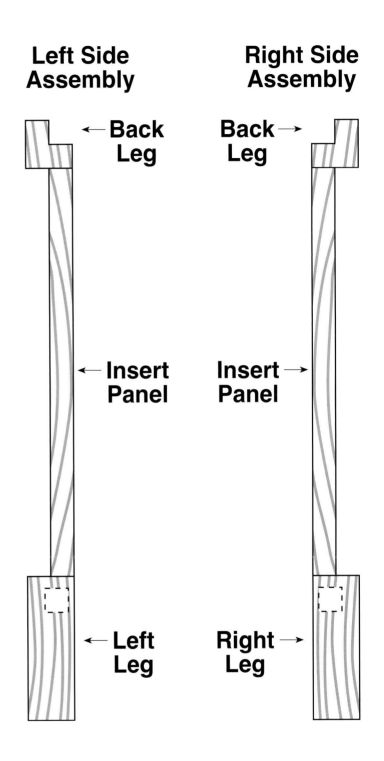

**Left Side Assembly**

**Right Side Assembly**

← **Back Leg**

**Back Leg** →

← **Insert Panel**

**Insert Panel** →

← **Left Leg**

**Right Leg** →

DRESSERS/CHESTS

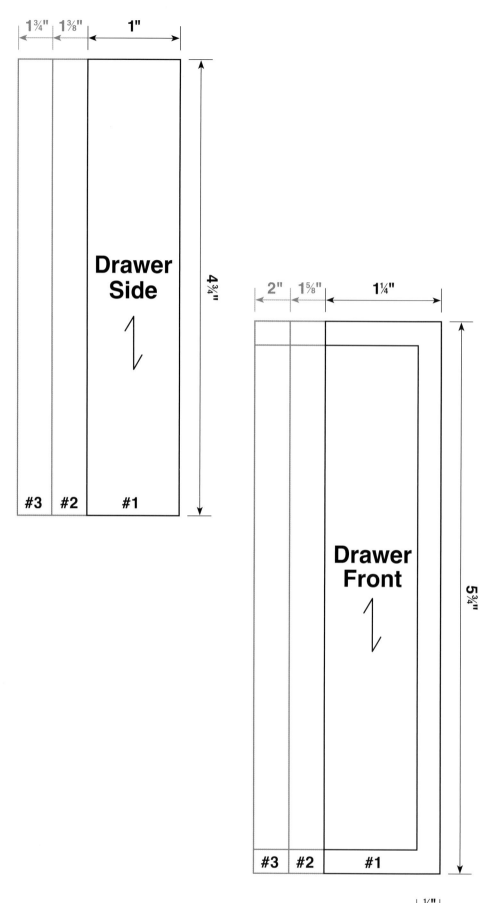

1¾"  1⅜"  1"

**Drawer
Side**

4¾"

#3  #2  #1

1¾"  1⅜"  1"

**Drawer
Back**

5¼"

#3  #2  #1

2"  1⅝"  1¼"

**Drawer
Front**

5¾"

#3  #2  #1

¼"

⅜"  ¼"

Shown actual size.

# *Armoire*

## Materials List

| Item | Width | Length | Thickness | Quantity | Wood Type | Location |
|------|-------|--------|-----------|----------|-----------|----------|
| Splat | 2" | 10¾" | ½" | 1 | Poplar | Page 114 |
| Top | 6¾" | 11¼" | ¼" | 1 | Poplar | |
| Case Top End | 5¾" | 10" | ¼" | 1 | Poplar | |
| Case Bottom & Center Shelf | 6" | 10" | ½" | 2 | Poplar | Page 111 |
| Case Back | 10½" | 17" | ¼" | 1 | Poplar | |
| Case Side | 6" | 17" | ½" | 2 | Poplar | Page 113 |
| Stile | ¾" | 17" | ½" | 2 | Poplar | Page 115 |
| Top Rail | ¾" | 9½" | ½" | 1 | Poplar | Page 115 |
| Drawer Bottom | 5½" | 9" | ¼" | 1 | Plywood | |
| Drawer Side | 2⅞" | 5½" | ¼" | 2 | Plywood | |
| Drawer Back | 2⅞" | 9" | ¼" | 1 | Plywood | |
| Drawer Front | 2⅞" | 9" | ¼" | 1 | Poplar | Page 112 |
| Door | 4¹¹⁄₁₆" | 12¼" | ¼" | 2 | Poplar | Page 112 |
| Door & Drawer Front Trim | ⅝" | 112" | ⅛" | 1 | Poplar | Page 115 |
| Base Front & Back | 1" | 11¼" | ⅜" | 1 | Poplar | Page 114 |
| Base Side | 1" | 6⅞" | ⅜" | 2 | Poplar | Page 114 |
| Rod Hanger | 2" | 5½" | ⅜" | 2 | Poplar | Page 115 |
| Rod | ¼" | 10" | | 1 | Dowel | |
| Hinge | ½" | ⅝" | | 4 | | |
| Wood Knob | | | ⅝" Dia. | 2 | | |

# Construction Sequence: Armoire

## Assembling the Case

1. Select hardwood materials of the proper thickness for each part.
2. Cut the Case Sides to the width and length specified on the drawing.
3. Cut the rabbet on the edge of the Case Side materials as specified on the drawing.
4. Cut the Case Back to the width and length specified.
5. Apply glue to the rabbet on the Case Sides and clamp the Case Sides to the Case Back. Ensure that the assembly is square.
6. Cut the Case Top End to the width and length specified.
7. Glue and clamp the Case Top End to the Case Assembly.
8. Cut a piece of ½"-thick wood, 4" wide and 27" long, to use in making the Stiles.

### Technical Note:

The Stile and the Top Rail pieces have a rabbet cut on the edge. The finished size of these pieces is ½" x ¼". These pieces would be too small to handle safely when cutting the rabbet. Using a wider board improves the safety of this operation.

9. Cut a ¼" x ¼" rabbet on both edges of this board.

10. Cut the Stiles and the Top Rail pieces from this board to the widths and lengths specified on the drawings.

11. Apply glue to the rabbet groove on the Stiles and clamp them to the Case Sides.

12. Cut the material for the Case Bottom & Center Shelf pieces to the width and length specified on drawing.

13. Cut ¼" x ½" notches in the two front corners where these pieces will fit with the Stiles. The Case Bottom & Center Shelf pieces will fit inside the assembly and will be flush with the front face of the Stiles.

14. Glue and clamp the Case Bottom to the Case Sides and the Case Back. Ensure that the Case Bottom is flush with bottom edges of the Case Assembly.

15. Mark the location of the Center Shelf, which is 3" from the Case Bottom.

16. Glue and clamp the Center Shelf to the Case Assembly. Ensure that the Center Shelf is aligned with the marks.

**Technical Note:**

Cut two short spacers from 3"-wide wood. Place these spacers against the Case Bottom to help ensure the alignment of the Center Shelf.

17. Cut the Top to the size specified.

18. Use a file and block sander to round over all the edges of the Top.

19. Apply glue to the Case End and clamp the Top to the Case Assembly. Ensure that the Top is centered on the width and length of the Case Assembly.

20. Cut Rod Hanger pieces to the size and shape specified on the drawing.

21. Drill ¼"-diameter holes in the Rod Hanger pieces.

22. Cut the Rod to a length of 10".

23. Glue and clamp the Rod and the Rod Hanger pieces to the inside of the Case Assembly.

24. Sand the Case Assembly to smooth out any imperfections caused during assembly.

## Making the Doors and the Trim Pieces

25. Cut the material for the Doors to the width and length specified on the drawing.

**Technical Note:**

The Door Front Trim on this project could be cut from individual pieces of wood and applied to the Doors to look more authentic. A simpler method is to cut the Door Front Trim pieces from a single piece of wood and attach them to the Doors as a single unit.

26. Cut approximately 112" of ⅛"-thick x ⅝"-wide wood for the Door & Drawer Front Trim.

27. Cut four Door Front Trim pieces 12¼" long.

28. Glue and clamp these Door Front Trim pieces to the edges of the two Doors.

29. Cut four Door Front Trim pieces for the tops and bottoms of the two Doors. Glue and clamp to the Doors.

**Technical Note:**

Photocopy the pattern for the Doors. Cut out the segment of the pattern for the top Door Front Trim piece. Use temporary adhesive to attach this pattern segment to a piece of scrap wood. Cut out the template and use it as a marking guide for the other Door Front Trim pieces.

DRESSERS/CHESTS

30. Test fit the trimmed Doors into the Door opening. Trim their widths or lengths if necessary.
31. Mark the locations for the Wood Knobs and attach them. They should be centered on the length of the Door and centered on the width of the Door Front Trim piece.
32. Mark the locations for the Hinges. These are located 1" in from the ends of both Doors.
33. Lay out and cut a mortise one-half the thickness of the folded hinge on the Doors.
34. Drill pilot holes and attach the Hinges to the Doors using #2 flat head screws.
35. Using the Hinges on the Doors as a guide, mark the locations on the Stiles where the Hinge mortises will be cut.
36. Cut the Hinge mortises in each Stile to one-half the thickness of the folded Hinge.
37. Drill pilot holes and attach the Hinges to the Doors using #2 flat head screws.

## Making the Drawers

38. Cut the material for the Drawer Side, the Drawer Back, the Drawer Front and the Drawer Bottom pieces.
39. Glue and clamp the Drawer pieces to each other to create a square Drawer.
40. Test fit the Drawer into the opening.
41. Cut the Drawer Front Trim pieces using the drawing as a guide. Glue and clamp the pieces to the drawer.

## Making the Base

42. Cut the materials for the Base Front, the Back and the Base Sides to the widths specified on the drawings.
43. Cut these pieces 2" longer than the drawings indicate.
44. Cut a 45-degree miter on the ends of each piece to fit these pieces around the Armoire Case Assembly.
45. Photocopy the drawing for the Base Front and the Base Side pieces. Use temporary adhesive to attach the photocopied pattern to these pieces and cut the decorative edges on these pieces.
46. Glue and clamp the Base Front, the Back and the Base Side pieces to the Armoire Case Assembly.

## Making the Splat

47. Photocopy the drawing for the Splat. Use temporary adhesive to attach the photocopy to an oversized board.
48. Cut the upper portion of the Splat. Leave the lower portion of the Splat attached to the oversized board.
49. Remove ⅛" from the thickness of the oversized board.
50. Cut the lower portion of the Splat from the oversized board.
51. Glue and clamp both parts of the Splat together. Ensure that the lower section of the Splat is flush with the back of the upper portion. This will create a ⅛" reveal on the front side of the Splat.
52. Glue and clamp the Splat to the Top. Set the Splat ⅜" back from the front edge of the Top. Center it on the width.

## Finishing

53. Sand the armoire and apply a finish.
54. This armoire would also look attractive made from walnut or cherry.
55. Miniature-sized stencils are available from arts and crafts stores.

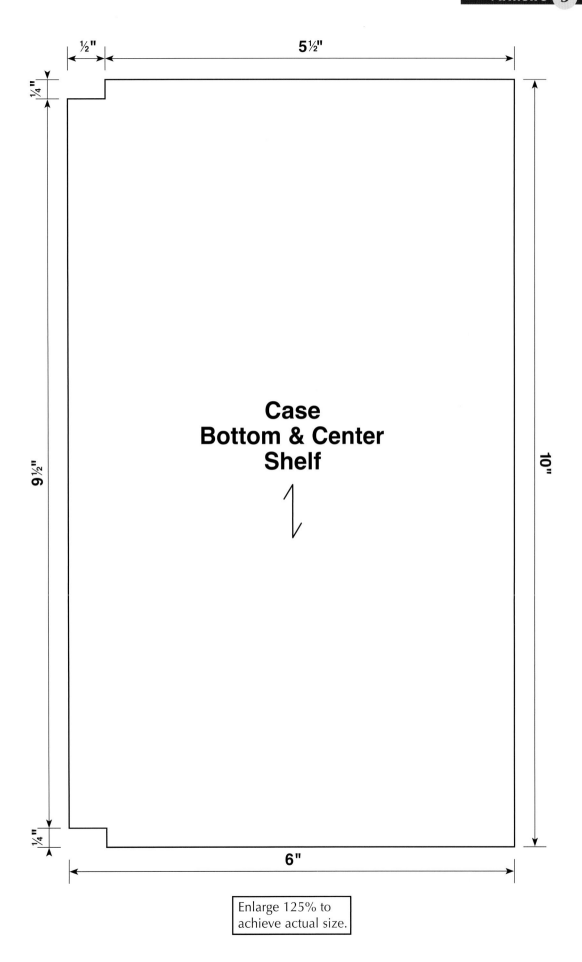

½"

5½"

¼"

9½"

10"

**Case
Bottom & Center
Shelf**

6"

¼"

Enlarge 125% to
achieve actual size.

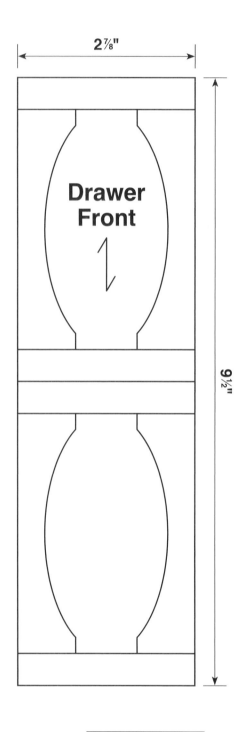

2⅞"

**Drawer
Front**

9½"

Enlarge 150% to
achieve actual size.

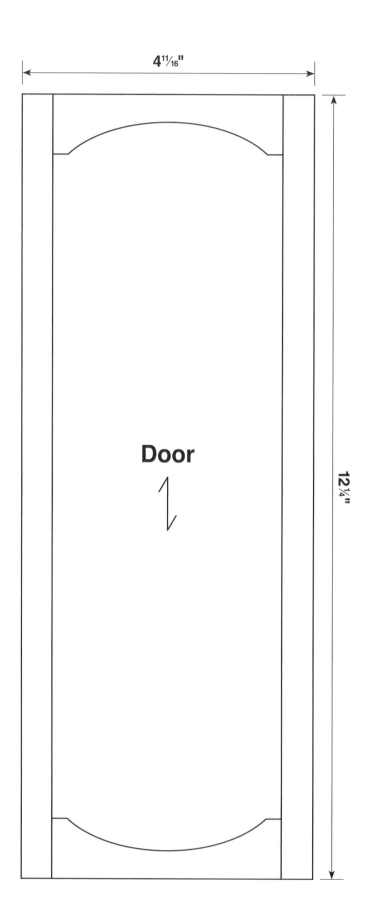

4¹¹⁄₁₆"

**Door**

12¼"

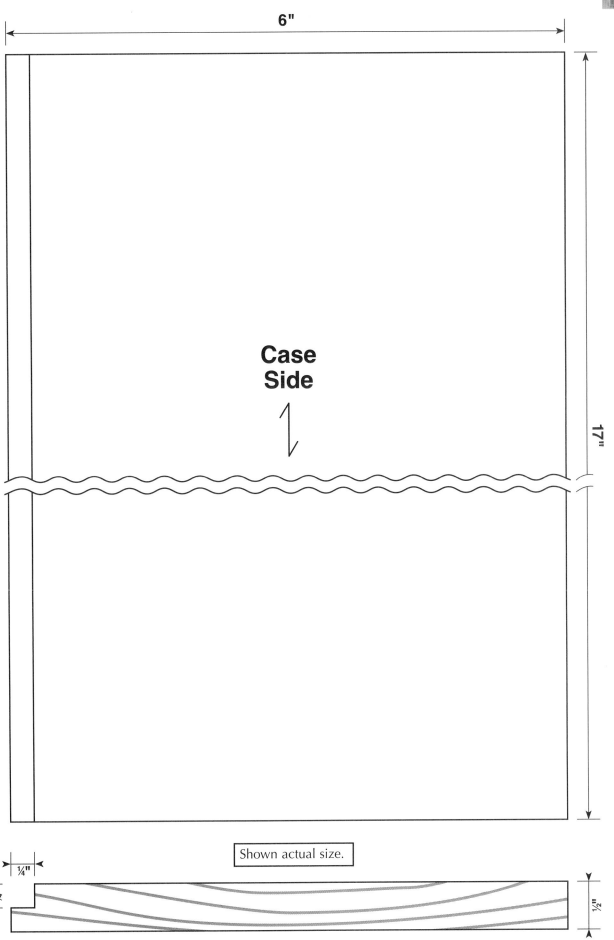

6"

**Case
Side**

17"

Shown actual size.

¼"

¼"

½"

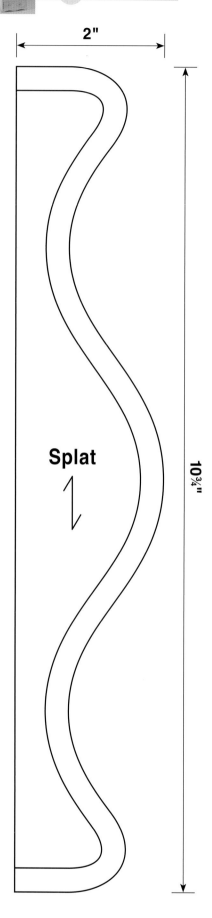

2"

**Splat**

10¾"

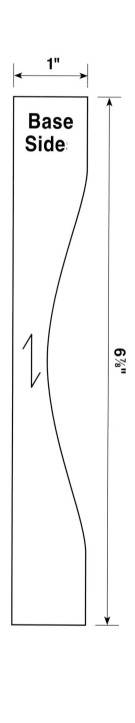

1"

**Base
Side**

6⅞"

Enlarge 125% to
achieve actual size.

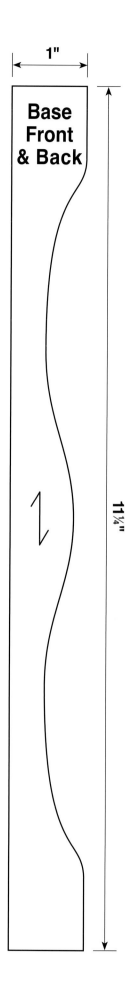

1"

**Base
Front
& Back**

11¼"

¾"

**Stile**

17"

¼"

¼"

½"

¾"

¾"

**Top
Rail**

9½"

¼"

¼"

½"

¾"

2"

**Rod
Hanger**

5½"

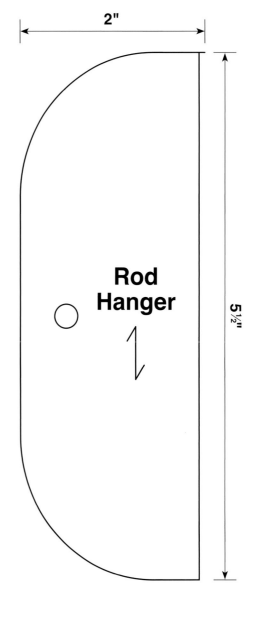

Shown actual size.

# Treasure Chest

## Materials List

| Item | Width | Length | Thickness | Quantity | Wood Type | Location |
|---|---|---|---|---|---|---|
| Top & Bottom | 4¾" | 12" | ½" | 2 | Birds eye | Page 118 |
| Side | 4¾" | 12" | ½" | 2 | Birds eye | Page 118 |
| End | 4¾" | 4¾" | ½" | 2 | Birds eye | Page 118 |
| Hinge | 1" | 12" | | 2 | Piano | |
| Hasp | | 1⁵⁄₁₆" | | 2 | Brass | |

# Construction Sequence: Treasure Chest

1. Select hardwood materials of the proper thickness for each part on the materials list.
2. Cut a board to 4¾" width and 60" long.
3. Cut a 45-degree miter edge on both edges of the board.
4. Cut two pieces to 4 ¾" length for the Ends.
5. Cut four pieces to 12" length for the Top & Bottom and the Sides.
6. Cut a 45-degree miter on the ends of each piece.

## Technical Note:

The miters on this project were cut using a table router. The router bit depth was set so the router bit would not cut the full thickness of the board. This left an unmitered area ⅛" thick. This technique leaves a decorative effect at the edges. The miters may be cut to their full thickness to attain a sharp corner miter joint, if desired.

7. Glue and clamp the Ends to the Sides. Ensure that the assembly is square.
8. Glue and clamp the Top & Bottom to the Sides. This makes a totally enclosed box.
9. Cut the box to separate the lid from the remainder of the box. The lid thickness should be 1½".
10. Mark the location for the piano Hinge on the inside edges of the lid and the chest.
11. Cut the mortises in the lid and chest pieces to half the thickness of the folded Hinge.
12. Sand the chest and apply a finish.
13. Install the Hinge.
14. Mark the location and install the Hasp 2½" from the Ends.
15. The treasure chest could be made with surface mount hinges. This would eliminate the mortising step.

4¾"

**Top,
Bottom
& Sides**

12"

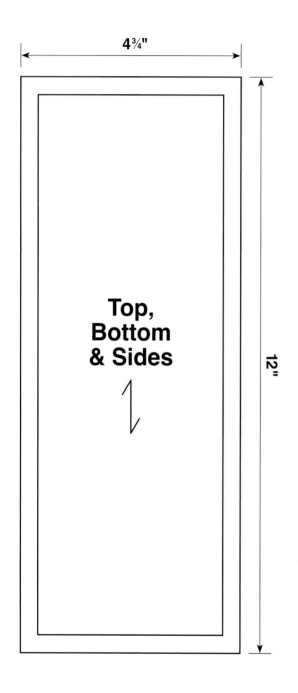

⅛"

4¾"

**End**

4¾"

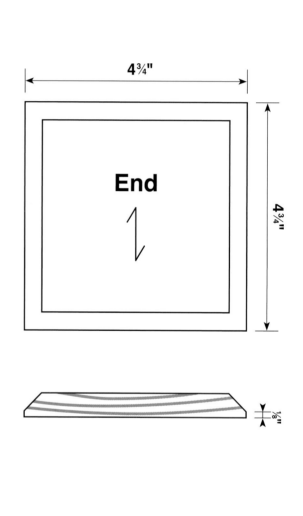

⅛"

Enlarge 200% to
achieve actual size.

# Part Six

# Doll Extras

I n addition to chairs, tables, beds and dressers, dolls need several other items to complete their surroundings. These items could conceivably include just about anything you see around you right now. For this book, I've zeroed in on four projects: a bookcase, a grandfather clock, a mirror and a school desk. Any one of these items will help to complete a room scene.

The bookcase, grandfather clock, and school desk are made with simple box construction techniques learned in the chapter on dressers and chests. The freestanding mirror requires the freehanded use of a router on small wood pieces. The owner's manual and other training materials should be consulted to learn how to safely do this. The dimensional and decorative shapes in the oval mirror frame are made using a router. Cutting the rabbet groove in the mirror frame to the proper depth for the mirror's thickness is critical on this project. The mirror glass is easily cut from acrylic mirror sheet stock using a scroll saw.

**Page 120**

**Page 123**

**Page 132**

**Page 140**

# Bookcase

## Materials List

| Item | Width | Length | Thickness | Quantity | Wood Type | Location |
|---|---|---|---|---|---|---|
| Side | 3" | 8½" | ⅜" | 2 | Walnut | Page 122 |
| Top | 3¼" | 6⅝" | ⅜" | 1 | Walnut | |
| Shelf | 2¾" | 5½" | ¼" | 4 | Walnut | |
| Back | 6" | 8½" | ¼" | 1 | Walnut | |
| Front | 1" | 5½" | ⅜" | 1 | Walnut | Page 122 |

# Construction Sequence: Bookcase

## Making the Sides and the Back

1. Select hardwood materials of the proper thickness for each bookcase part.
2. Cut a board 17" long and 3" wide for the Sides.
3. Cut a ¼" x ¼" rabbet on the edge of this board.
4. Cut the Side materials to the 8½" length specified on the drawing.
5. Cut the Back piece to the size specified on the materials list.
6. Apply glue to the rabbet groove in the Sides and assemble the Sides with the Back. Clamp the assembly until the glue is dry. Ensure that the assembly is square.

## Making the Shelves

7. Cut the four Shelves to the length and width specified on the materials list.
8. Cut the Front piece to the size specified on the drawing.
9. Photocopy the pattern for the Front piece. Use temporary adhesive to attach the photocopy to the wood piece for the Front and cut the decorative edge.
10. Apply glue to the top edge of the Front and clamp flush with the front edge of one of the Shelves.
11. Apply glue to three edges of the Bottom Shelf Assembly. Clamp this to the Bookcase Assembly.
12. Apply glue to all edges of the Top Shelf. Clamp flush with the top edge of the Bookcase Assembly. The Top Shelf is an end to the Shelf Assembly and a large surface for gluing the Top piece to the Bookcase Assembly.
13. Glue and clamp the Center Shelves to the Bookcase Assembly. Space the Upper Center Shelf 1½" down from the Top Shelf. Space the Lower Center Shelf 2½" up from the Bottom Shelf.

### Technical Note:

Use two short pieces of scrap wood, 1½" wide each, to align the Upper Center Shelf before clamping. Use two pieces of wood, 2½" wide each, as spacers for the Lower Center Shelf.

14. Sand the Bookcase Assembly to dress up any imperfections incurred during the assembly process.

## Making the Top

15. Cut the wood for the Top piece to the width and length specified on the materials list.
16. Glue and clamp the Top onto the Bookcase Assembly. Center the Top with the bookcase width and flush with the Back.

## Finishing

17. Sand the bookcase and apply a finish.

EXTRAS

3"

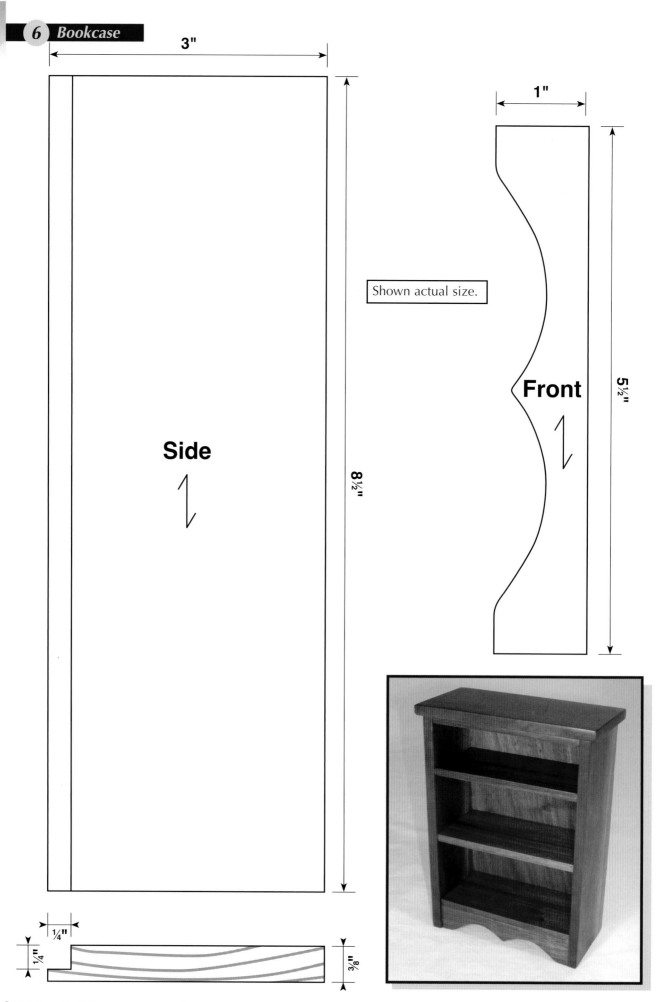

**Side**

8½"

1"

Shown actual size.

**Front**

5½"

¼"

¼"

⅜"

# Grandfather Clock

## Materials List

| Item | Width | Length | Thickness | Quantity | Wood Type | Location |
|---|---|---|---|---|---|---|
| **Top Case** | | | | | | |
| Front | 5½" | 5½" | ¼" | 1 | Walnut | Page 130 |
| Side | 3" | 5½" | ⅜" | 2 | Walnut | Page 129 |
| Back | 5¼" | 5½" | ¼" | 1 | Walnut | |
| Top & Bottom | 3¾" | 6" | ¼" | 2 | Walnut | |
| Front Accent | 4½" | 4½" | ⅛" | 1 | Cherry | Page 129 |
| Splat | 1½" | 6" | ⅜" | 1 | Walnut | Page 130 |
| Decorative Carving | 1⅛" | 5⅜" | | 1 | | |
| **Center Case** | | | | | | |
| Door | 4⅜" | 11⅞" | ¼" | 1 | Walnut | |
| Accent Door | 3¹⁄₁₆" | 10½" | ⅛" | 1 | Cherry | |
| Side | 3" | 12" | ⅜" | 2 | Walnut | Page 131 |
| Back | 4⅛" | 12" | ¼" | 1 | Walnut | |
| End | 2¾" | 3⅝" | ¼" | 1 | Walnut | |
| Hinge | ½" | ⅝" | | 2 | | |
| Wood Knob | | | ⅝" Dia. | 1 | | |
| **Base** | | | | | | |
| Front | 1¾" | 5⅝" | ¾" | 1 | Cherry | Page 127 |
| Side | 1¾" | 4" | ¾" | 2 | Cherry | Page 128 |
| Top | 3½" | 5" | ¼" | 1 | Walnut | Page 127 |
| Clock Works | | | 2¾" Fit-up | 1 | | |

# Construction Sequence: Grandfather Clock

## Assembling the Top Case

1. Select hardwood materials of the proper thickness for each clock part.
2. Cut the Side material to the width and length specified on drawing.
3. Cut a ¼" x ¼" rabbet on the edge of the material for the Sides.
4. Cut the material for the Back to the width and length specified on the drawing.
5. Apply glue to the rabbet groove on the Sides. Assemble the Sides with the Back and clamp them together until the glue is dry. Ensure that the assembly is square.
6. Cut the material for the Front to the size specified on the drawing.
7. Lay out and cut the clock's 2⅜"-diameter hole in the center of the Front. The hole can be cut on a scroll saw or by using a Fostner bit in a drill press.
8. Apply glue to the front edges of the Sides and clamp the Front to the assembly.
9. Sand the assembly to dress up any imperfections that occurred during the assembly.
10. Photocopy the pattern for the Accent Front. Use temporary adhesive and attach the photocopied pattern to the wood piece selected for the Accent Front. Cut the Accent Front, following the pattern lines, and cut the 2⅜" clock hole.
11. Glue and clamp the Accent Front to the Front.

12. Cut the Top & Bottom to the size specified on the drawing.
13. Using a file and block sander, round over the front length and the two sides of the Top & Bottom pieces.
14. Apply glue to the top edge of the Top Case Assembly. Glue and clamp the Top to the assembly. Use the same procedure to attach the Bottom to the assembly. Center the Top & Bottom on the width of the assembly and make sure that it is flush with the Back.
15. Photocopy the Splat pattern. Use temporary adhesive to attach the photocopy to the Splat and cut this piece.
16. Glue and clamp the Decorative Carving to the Splat.
17. Glue the Splat to the top of the assembly. Center it on the length of the Top, set back ⅜" from the rounded front edge.

## Assembling the Center Case
18. Cut the Side material to the width and length specified on drawing.
19. Cut a ¼" x ¼" rabbet on the edge of the material for the Sides.
20. Cut the material for the Back to width and length specified on the drawing.
21. Apply glue to the rabbet groove on the Sides. Assemble the Sides with the Back and clamp these parts until the glue is dry. Ensure that the assembly is square.
22. Cut the End for the Center Case Assembly.
23. Glue and clamp the End to the assembly.
24. Sand the Center Case Assembly to dress up any imperfections from the assembly process.
25. Cut the materials for the Door and the Accent Door to the sizes specified on the materials list.
26. Glue and clamp the Accent Door to the Door. Center the Accent Door on the Door.
27. Lay out the locations for the Hinges 1½" from the ends of the Door.
28. Drill the Hinge holes and attach the Hinges to the Door using flat head screws.
29. Mark the location of the Hinges on the Center Case Assembly using the Door as a guide.
30. Cut a mortise into the side panel of the Center Case Assembly equal to the thickness of the folded Hinge. These Hinge mortises can be cut using a fret saw and a wood chisel.
31. Drill the Hinge hole location to attach the Door Assembly to the Center Case Assembly. **Do not install the Door at this time.**
32. Drill the hole in the Door for the Wood Knob. Glue and clamp the Knob to the Door.
33. Glue and clamp the Center Case Assembly to the Top Case Assembly. Ensure that the Center Case Assembly is centered on the width of the Top Case Assembly and that the Backs are flush.

## Assembling the Base
34. Cut a ¾"-thick board to the width specified on the drawing for the Front and Sides. The length of the board should be approximately 20". Do not cut this board into shorter pieces at this time.
35. Cut a ⅜" x ¼" rabbet on the edge of the 20"-long board.
36. Use a router with a ¼" radius cove bit to cut the edge opposite the rabbet on the 20"-long board.
37. Cut a 45-degree miter on each end of the Front piece for the base. The length specified on the drawing is approximate.
38. Cut a 45-degree miter on one end and cut to the length specified on the drawing for the left and right Sides.
39. Dry assemble the Front piece with the Sides. Measure the inside area of the rabbets where the Top piece will fit to determine the final size for the Top piece.
40. Cut the base Top to the size indicated on the drawing (adjusting the dimensions according to the measurements in the previous step).
41. Photocopy the pattern for the Front. Use a temporary adhesive to attach the photocopy to the Front. Cut the decorative shape on the bottom of the Front piece.
42. Apply glue to the miter corners and rabbet. Assemble the Sides, the Front and the Top pieces and clamp the assembly.

43. Cut a piece of wood to fill in the back of the Base Assembly. Glue and clamp the filler piece flush with the back edge of the Base Assembly.
44. Sand the Base Assembly to dress up any imperfections from the assembly process.
45. Glue and clamp the Base Assembly to the Center Case Assembly. Ensure that the Center Case Assembly is centered on the width of the Base Assembly and that the Backs are flush.

## Final Assembly and Finishing
46. Install the Door onto the Center Case Assembly using flat head screws to attach the Hinges.
47. Test the Door movement and adjust the length, if necessary.
48. Sand the clock and apply a finish.

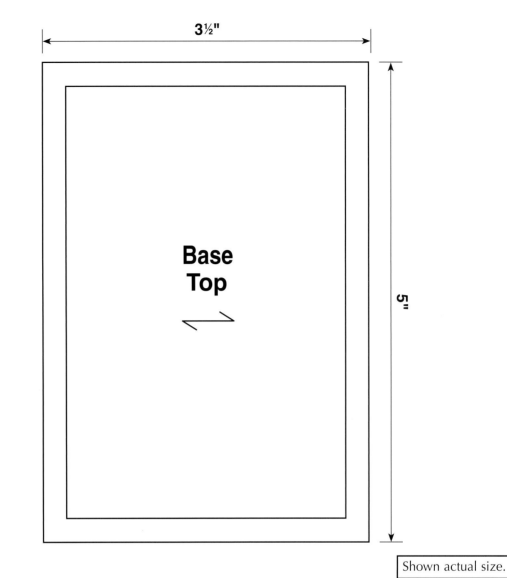

**Base Top**

3½"

5"

Shown actual size.

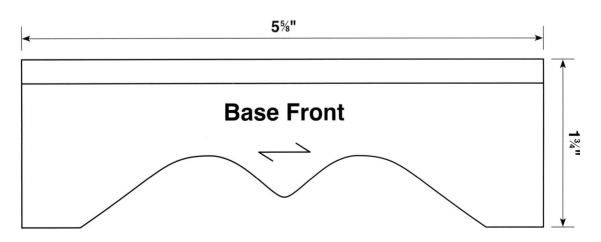

**Base Front**

5⅝"

1¾"

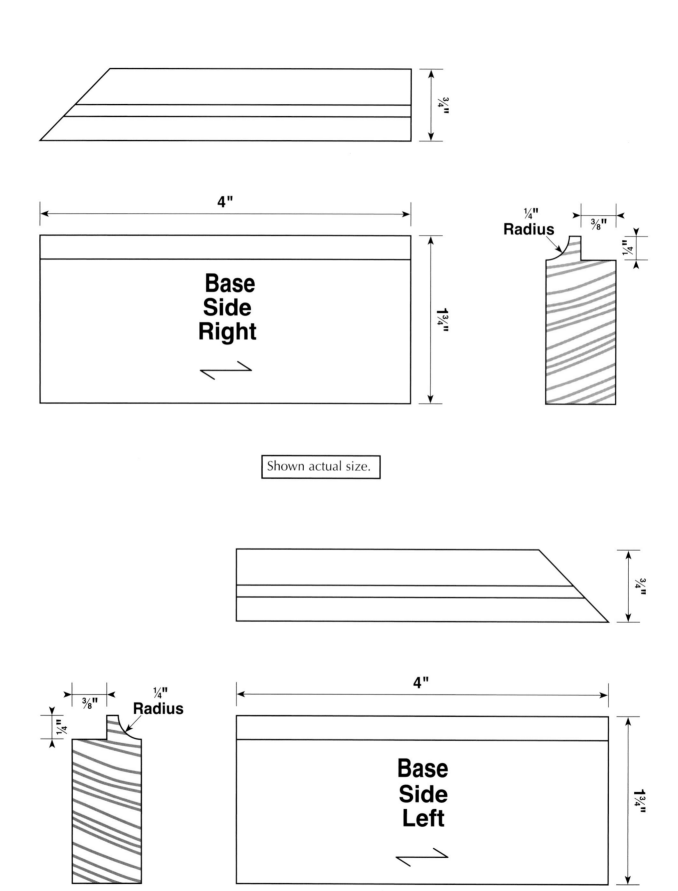

3/4"

4"

**Base
Side
Right**

1/4"
**Radius**

3/8"

1/4"

1³/4"

Shown actual size.

3/4"

1/4"
3/8"
**Radius**

1/4"

4"

**Base
Side
Left**

1³/4"

5½"

3"

**Top Case
Side**

3/8"

¼"

¼"

Shown actual size.

4½"

**Front
Accent**

**Hole
2⅜" Diameter**

4½"

3/4"
**Radius**

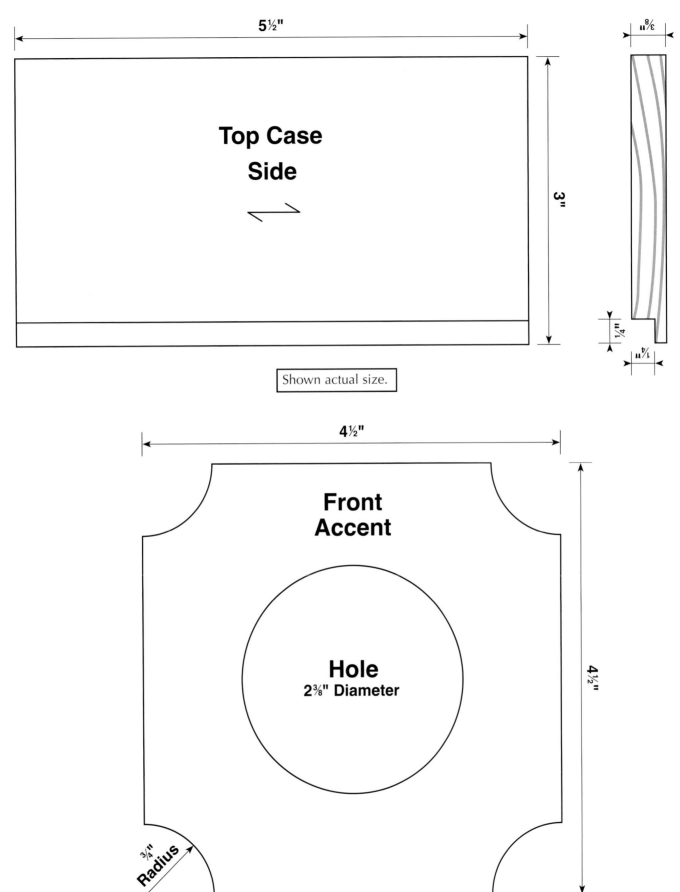

EXTRAS

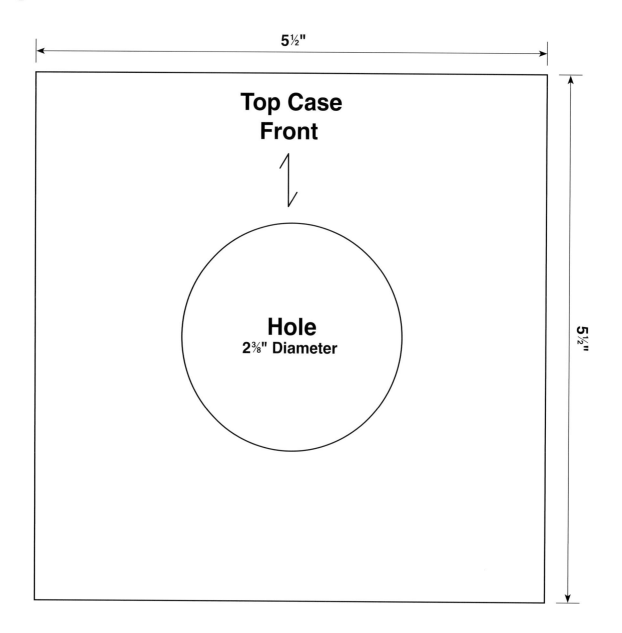

5½"

5½"

**Top Case
Front**

**Hole
2⅜" Diameter**

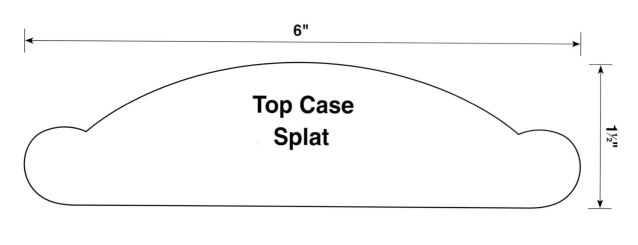

6"

1½"

**Top Case
Splat**

Shown actual size.

3"

12"

**Center
Case
Side**

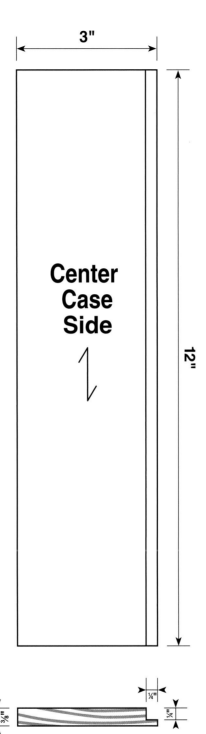

3/8"

1/4"

1/4"

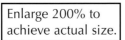

Enlarge 200% to
achieve actual size.

# *Mirror*

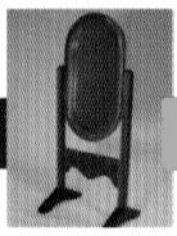

## Materials List

| Item | Width | Length | Thickness | Quantity | Wood Type | Location |
|---|---|---|---|---|---|---|
| Frame | 6" | 10½" | ¾" | 1 | Cherry | Page 138 |
| Back Cover | 5½" | 10" | ⅛" | 1 | Plywood | Page 136 |
| Stretcher | 2½" | 7" | ⅜" | 1 | Walnut | Page 139 |
| Leg | ½" | 11½" | ½" | 2 | Walnut | Page 137 |
| Foot | ¾" | 6" | ¾" | 2 | Walnut | Page 137 |
| Acrylic Mirror | 5" | 9½" | ⅛" | 1 | Acrylic | Page 135 |
| Decorative Carving | 3¼" | 1½" | | 1 | | |
| Round Head Screw | | 1¼" | #6 | 2 | | |

# Construction Sequence: Mirror

1. Select hardwood materials of the proper thickness for each part on the materials list.
2. Photocopy the drawing for the Frame piece. Attach the photocopy to an oversized piece of wood (6½" x 12") for the Frame.
3. Cut out the center hole in the Frame.
4. Sand the surfaces of the center hole to smooth out any imperfections from the saw blade.
5. Use a router with a pilot-guided rabbet bit to cut the ⅛"-deep rabbet around the center hole.
6. Use a router with a pilot-guided ⅜" cove bit to cut the decorative cove groove on the front side of the Frame.
7. Cut the outside dimensions of the Frame, following the lines on the photocopy.
8. Sand the outside surfaces to smooth out any imperfections from the saw blade.
9. Use a router with a pilot-guided ⅜" cove bit to cut the decorative groove on the outside of the Frame.
10. Photocopy the drawing for the Acrylic Mirror. Use temporary adhesive to attach the photocopy to the Acrylic Mirror. Cut the Mirror, following the lines on the photocopy.
11. Test fit the Acrylic Mirror in the Frame. Adjust the size, if necessary. Set the Acrylic Mirror in a safe place; it will be installed later in the sequence of construction.
12. Photocopy the drawing for the Back Cover. Use temporary adhesive to attach the photocopy to the ⅛" plywood and cut out the Back Cover.
13. Cut the pieces for the Leg, the Foot and the Stretcher pieces.
14. Lay out and cut the tenons on the ends of the Stretcher and the two Leg pieces as specified on the drawings.
15. Lay out the mortise locations in the two Leg pieces, following the dimensions on the drawing.
16. Use a ¼" mortise bit to drill the mortise holes ¼" deep in the Leg pieces.
17. Use a file or a sanding block to make the decorative top on the Leg pieces. This is a 22-degree angle cut on four sides.
18. Lay out and drill clearance holes for the #6 Round Head Screws that will serve as the support for the Frame.
19. Lay out mortises in the two Foot pieces. Use a ¼" mortise bit to drill the mortises ⅜" deep.
20. Dry fit the tenon on each Leg to the mortises in the Foot pieces.
21. Dry fit the tenons on the Stretcher with the mortises in the Leg pieces.
22. Drill screw pilot holes for the #6 Round Head Screws in the Frame side. The holes should be centered on the height and thickness of the Frame.
23. Test fit the Frame into the Leg Support Assembly.
24. Disassemble all of the pieces.

25. Apply wood glue to the tenons on the Leg pieces and the mortises in the Foot pieces. Assemble and clamp until dry.
26. Apply wood glue to the Decorative Carving and clamp it to the Stretcher. Ensure that the Decorative Carving is centered on the Stretcher.
27. Glue the tenons on the Stretcher to mortises in the Leg pieces. Clamp. Ensure that the assembly is square.
28. Sand all the surfaces and apply a finish to the front and the sides of the Frame piece. **Do not put any finish on the backside of the mirror Frame at this time.**
29. Apply a finish to the Leg Support Assembly.
30. When all the coats of finish have dried, install the Acrylic Mirror and Back Cover.
31. Remove the protective vinyl sheet from the Acrylic Mirror. Place the Acrylic Mirror in the Frame.
32. Apply glue and clamp the Back Cover to the Frame. Ensure that the Back Cover is centered on the Frame.
33. Apply a finish to the Back Cover and to the back of the Frame. Ensure that no finish gets on the Acrylic Mirror because it may damage the acrylic plastic surface.
34. Mount the Frame Assembly in the Leg Support Assembly using two #6 Round Head Screws.

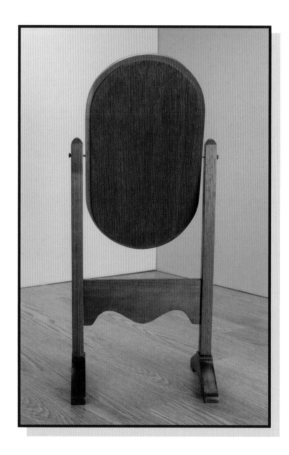

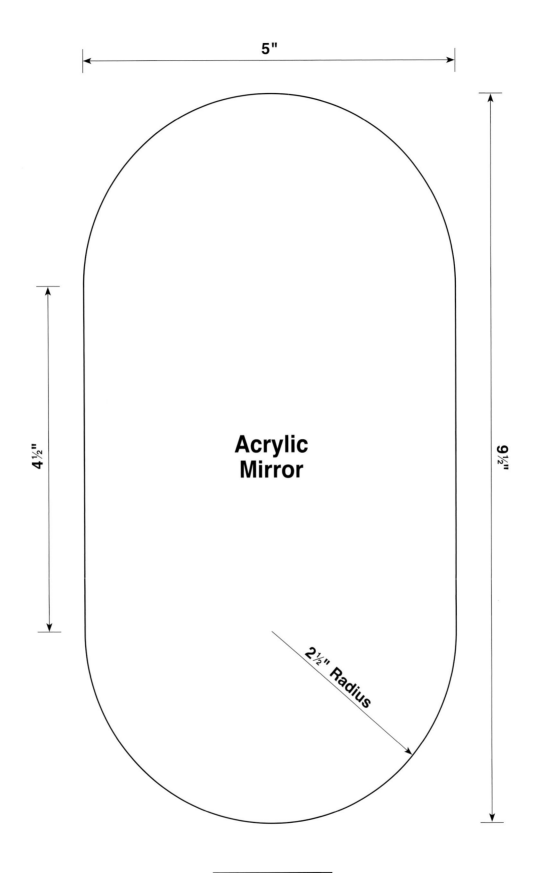

5"

9½"

4½"

**Acrylic
Mirror**

2½" Radius

Enlarge 125% to
achieve actual size.

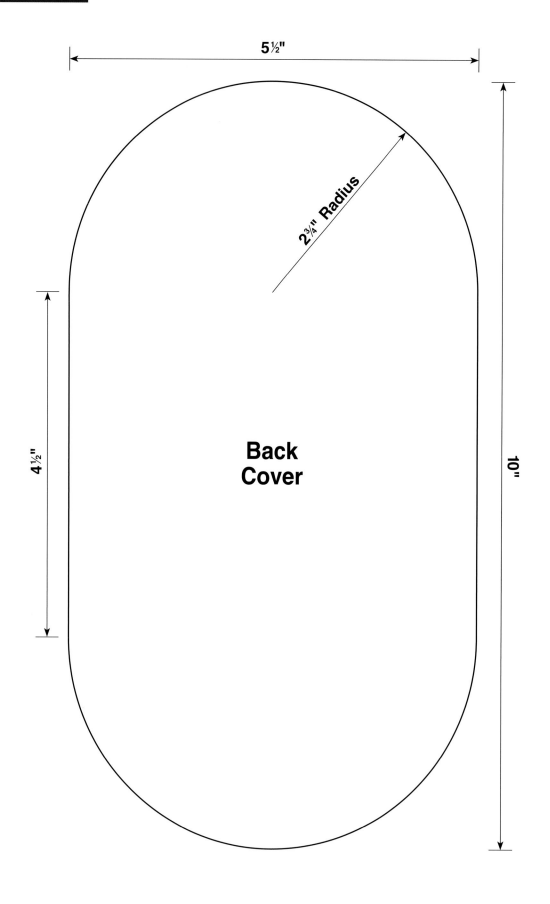

5½"

2¾" Radius

4½"

10"

**Back
Cover**

Enlarge 125% to
achieve actual size.

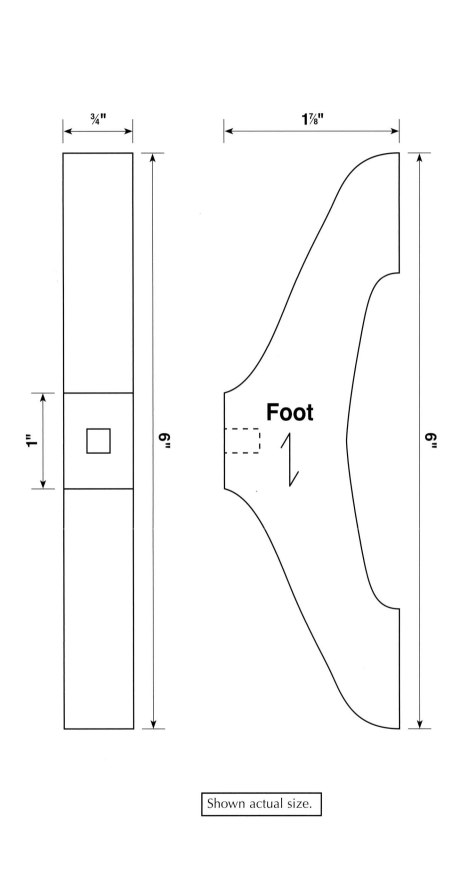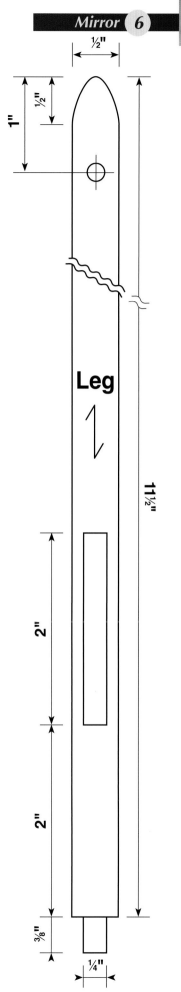

# Mirror 6

¾"

1⅞"

1"

6"

6"

**Foot**

Shown actual size.

½"

½"

1"

**Leg**

11½"

2"

2"

⅜"

¼"

EXTRAS

Making Doll Furniture in Wood ● 137

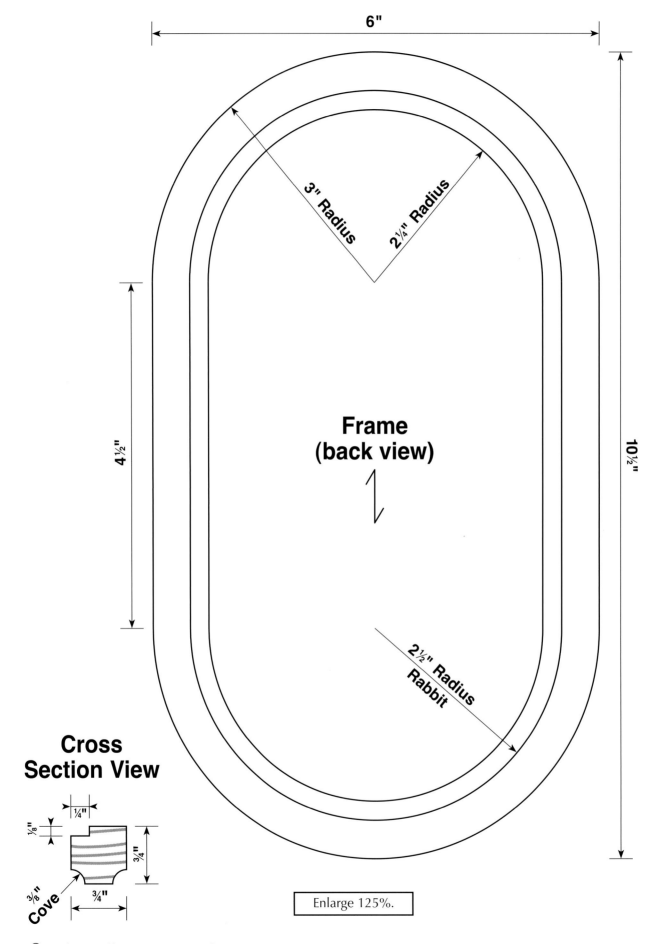

6"

10½"

4½"

3" Radius

2¼" Radius

**Frame
(back view)**

2½" Radius
Rabbit

**Cross
Section View**

¼"

⅛"

¾"

⅜"
**Cove**

¾"

Enlarge 125%.

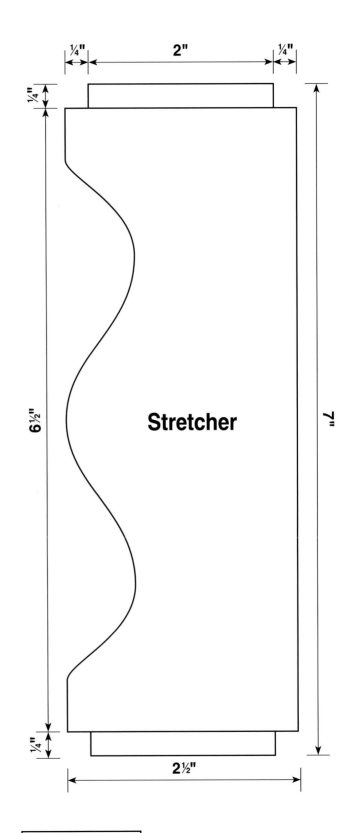

**Stretcher**

Shown actual size.

# *School Desk*

## Materials List

| Item | Width | Length | Thickness | Quantity | Wood Type | Location |
|------|-------|--------|-----------|----------|-----------|----------|
| Desk Leg | 5½" | 5 ½" | ½" | 2 | Poplar | Page 145 |
| Support Stretcher | 2½" | 5½" | ½" | 2 | Poplar | Page 145 |
| Desk Top Wide | 4⅛" | 7" | ⅜" | 1 | Poplar | Page 146 |
| Desk Top Narrow | 1⅞" | 7" | ⅜" | 1 | Poplar | Page 144 |
| Desk Case Side | 2¼" | 5⅜" | ⅜" | 2 | Poplar | Page 144 |
| Desk Case Front | 1⅛" | 6" | ⅜" | 1 | Poplar | |
| Desk Case Back | 2¼" | 6" | ⅜" | 1 | Poplar | |
| Desk Case Floor | 6" | 7" | ⅜" | 1 | Poplar | |
| Seat Side | 5½" | 8⅝" | ½" | 2 | Poplar | Page 143 |
| Seat | 4½" | 5½" | ⅜" | 1 | Poplar | |
| Seat Back | 4" | 5½" | ⅜" | 1 | Poplar | |
| Hinge | ½" | ⅝" | | 2 | Brass | |

# Construction Sequence: School Desk

## Cutting

1. Select hardwood materials of the proper thickness for each part on the materials list.
2. Photocopy the patterns for the Desk Legs, the Support Stretchers and the Seat Sides.
3. Use temporary adhesive to attach the photocopies to the wood pieces selected for these parts.
4. Drill saw blade pilot holes for all the inside cuts on the Desk Leg, the Support Stretcher and the Seat Side parts.
5. Cut out all these pieces using a scroll saw.
6. Rough-sand all the pieces to remove any saw marks and wood burrs.

## Assembling the Desk Case

7. Lay out and cut all the pieces to the sizes specified on the drawings for the Desk Case Sides, the Desk Case Front, the Desk Case Back, the Desk Top Wide, the Desk Top Narrow and the Desk Case Floor.
8. Cut a 16-degree angle on one edge of the Desk Top Wide, as specified on the drawing.
9. Lay out the location for the Hinges on the Desk Top Wide and the Desk Top Narrow pieces. The Hinges are located ½" in from the ends as shown on the drawing. Cut a mortise groove on both Top pieces. The mortise is the length of the Hinge and half the thickness of the folded Hinge.
10. Mark the Hinge hole locations and drill pilot holes. Install the Hinges to join both Top pieces using #2 flat head wood screws.

### Technical Note:

If a micro-sized pilot twist drill is not available, use a small brad nail as a substitute.

11. Round over the edges of the Desk Top Assembly and the Desk Case Floor. **Do not round over the edges with the Hinges.** Use a file and sanding block to round over the edges.

12. Glue and clamp the Desk Case Sides to the Desk Case Front and the Desk Case Back pieces. Ensure that the assembly is square.
13. Apply glue to the bottom edges of the Desk Case Assembly and clamp it to the Desk Case Floor. Center the Desk Case Floor on the Desk Case Assembly.
14. Glue and clamp the Desk Top Narrow piece to the Desk Case Assembly. Ensure that the Hinge edge of the Desk Top Narrow is aligned with the point where the Desk Case Sides begin to slope.
15. Sand the Desk Case Assembly.
16. Glue and clamp one of the Support Stretchers between two of the Desk Legs. The glue point is noted on the drawing of the Desk Legs. Ensure that the top edge of the Support Stretcher is flush with the top edges of the Desk Legs and that the assembly is square.
17. Glue the Desk Case Assembly to the Desk Leg Assembly. Center the Desk Leg Assembly on the Desk Case Floor.

## Assembling the Desk Seat

18. Cut the Seat and the Seat Back pieces to the sizes specified on the materials list. Ensure that the length of the Support Stretcher and the length of the Seat and Seat Back pieces are the same.
19. Round over the edges of the Seat and the Seat Back. Use a file and a sanding block to round over the edges. Do not round over the ends of these pieces.
20. Glue and clamp the Seat, the Seat Back and the Support Stretcher to the Seat Sides. Ensure that the clamped assembly is square.

## Finish

21. Sand all the wood surfaces.
22. Apply a stain and a finish to the Seat, the Seat Back and the Desk Case Assembly.
23. Paint the Legs of the Desk and the Seat Assemblies with rusty brown acrylic craft paint.

**5½"**

Shown actual size.

**8⅝"**

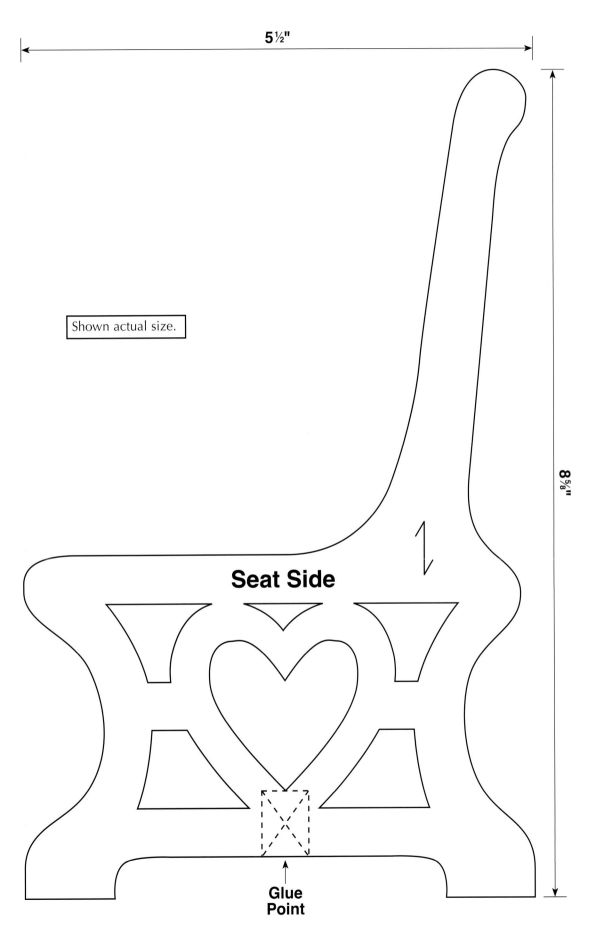

**Seat Side**

**Glue Point**

½" ⅝" **Hinge Mortise** ⅝" ½"

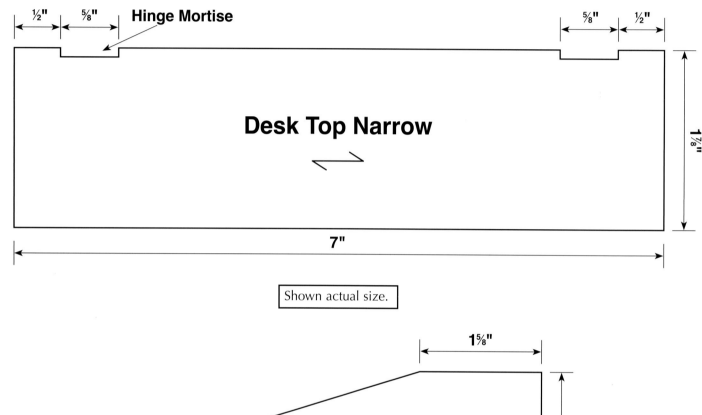

**Desk Top Narrow**

1⅞"

7"

Shown actual size.

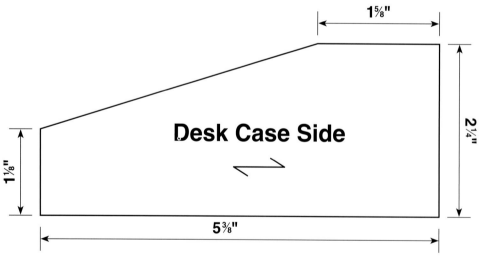

1⅝"

**Desk Case Side**

2¼"

1⅛"

5⅜"

Enlarge 125% to
achieve actual size.

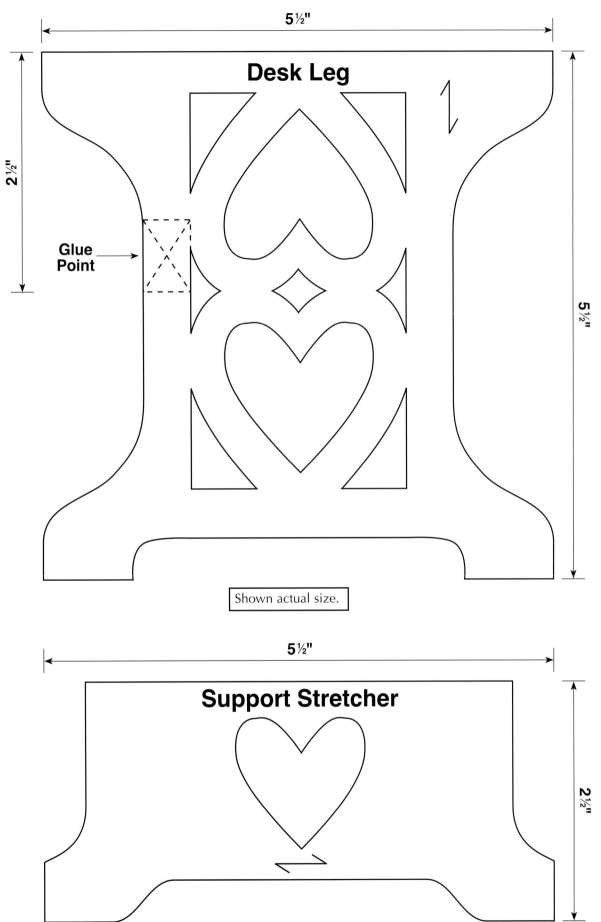

5½"

**Desk Leg**

2½"

5½"

**Glue Point**

Shown actual size.

5½"

**Support Stretcher**

2½"

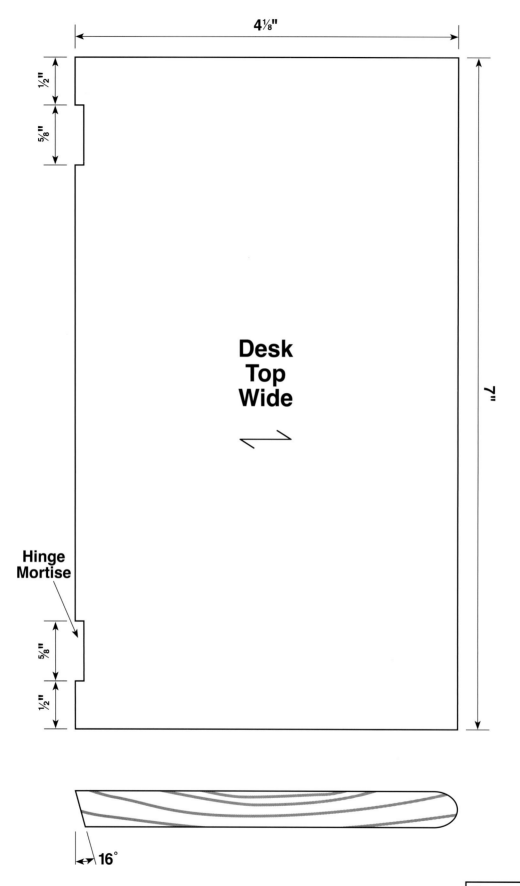

4⅛"

½"

⅝"

**Desk
Top
Wide**

7"

**Hinge
Mortise**

⅝"

½"

16°

Shown actual size.

# Part Seven

# Doll Traveling Cases

*Page 148*

*Page 156*

*Page 162*

As a final part in this book of doll furniture, I have included several items that are not necessarily furniture. However, these items can be made with all of the woodworking tools and techniques used in the previous chapters. They are storage cases, and they will help to keep any collector's—young and old alike—collection of dolls organized and securely stored when not on display or in use.

Here in this chapter you will find four traveling cases designed especially for 18" dolls: a hope chest, a Southwestern-style trunk, a traveling case and a classic trunk.

The box making methods learned in the previous chapters will help you construct all these projects. The traveling case requires the application of a heavy weight wall covering. The manufacturer's directions should be followed when gluing the paper onto the traveling case. A fabric material could be substituted for the wall covering if excessive handling is likely to occur.

*Page 168*

# *Hope Chest*

## Materials List

| Item | Width | Length | Thickness | Quantity | Wood Type | Location |
|---|---|---|---|---|---|---|
| Front & Back | 11" | 24" | ½" | 2 | Walnut | Page 153 |
| End | 11" | 12¾" | ½" | 2 | Walnut | Page 151 |
| Bottom | 12¾" | 23½" | ½" | 1 | Walnut | |
| Lid Wide | 9½" | 24¾" | ½" | 1 | Walnut | |
| Lid Narrow | 4" | 24¾" | ½" | 1 | Walnut | |
| Splat | 3" | 24" | ½" | 1 | Walnut | Page 155 |
| Decorative Piece | 2¼" | 7" | ¼" | 1 | Cherry | Page 154 |
| Foot | 3¼" | 3¼" | ¾" | 4 | Walnut | Page 152 |
| Hinge | 1⅜" | 2" | | 2 | | |
| Lid Support | | 7" | | 1 | | |

## Construction Sequence: Hope Chest

1. Purchase ½"-thick walnut for this project.
2. Cut the Bottom and the End pieces to the sizes specified on the drawings and the materials list.
3. Cut a ½" x ¼" rabbet on all the edges of the End and the Front & Back pieces as specified on the drawings.
4. Apply glue to the rabbet cuts on the Front & Back pieces where the Ends will join. Clamp the assembly. Ensure that the rabbet cuts in the End pieces are oriented in the same direction as the rabbet grooves on the Front & Back pieces. Ensure that the assembly is square.
5. Cut the Bottom piece to the size specified on the materials list.
6. Apply glue to the rabbet cuts in the End and in the Front & Back pieces. Insert the Bottom piece and clamp these pieces to complete the assembly.
7. Select a ¾" board to be used to make the Foot pieces. Do not cut the Foot pieces to size yet. Cut a board that is 6½" x 6½" in size. Use a router with a ¼" Roman Ogee bit to cut the decorative edge on all of the edges of this board. Cut the Foot pieces to the dimensions indicated on the materials list.
8. Mark the locations on the Foot pieces where they will align with the corners of the Box Assembly. These will be set out from the corner ¾" on both edges. Apply glue to the Foot pieces and clamp them to the Box Assembly. Screws could be used to supplement this attachment, if desired.
9. Cut the Lid Wide and the Lid Narrow pieces to the sizes specified on the drawing and the materials list.
10. Measure and mark the location where the Lid Narrow will fit to the Box Assembly. This piece is flush with the Back and centered on the length of the Box Assembly.
11. Mark the locations along the joining edges and drill pilot holes for the 1¼" finishing brad nails. Use two on each end and three along the back.
12. Apply glue on the top edge of the Box Assembly where these pieces will join. Attach the Lid Narrow to the Box Assembly using the brad nails. Clamp this assembly until the glue is dry. Use a nail set to countersink the nail heads below the wood surface. Use wood filler to hide these nail heads.
13. Select the wood to be used for the Splat. Ensure that the edge of this board is straight. Use a wood plane or jointer to straighten this edge, if necessary.
14. Photocopy the pattern for the Splat. Use temporary adhesive to attach the photocopy to the Splat. Cut the profile using a scroll saw, band saw or jigsaw.

15. Select the wood for the Decorative Piece. Photocopy the pattern for this piece. Use temporary adhesive to attach the photocopy to the Decorative Piece. Cut the profile using a scroll saw, band saw or jigsaw.
16. Use a woodcarving gouge to cut the relief areas of the Decorative Piece to create the rising sun decoration. Sand and smooth all of the edges and grooves.
17. Mark the location on the Splat where the Decorative Piece will be attached. Apply glue to the backside of the Decorative Piece and clamp it to the Splat.
18. Mark the location where the Splat will be attached to the Lid Narrow. This will be inset from the back edge by ¼". Mark the location for the three screws, centered where the Splat will attach and spaced with one in the center and two others 7" out from the center.
19. Drill pilot holes for the #4 screws in the Lid Narrow and mating holes in the edge of the Splat.
20. Apply glue to the edge of the Splat and use 1"-long screws to attach it to the Top.
21. Lay the Lid Wide in place on the Box Assembly. Mark the location for the Hinges 4" in from each end. Drill pilot holes matching the Hinges. Attach the Hinges to complete the assembly of the hope chest.
22. Sand the chest, inside and out, and apply a finish.

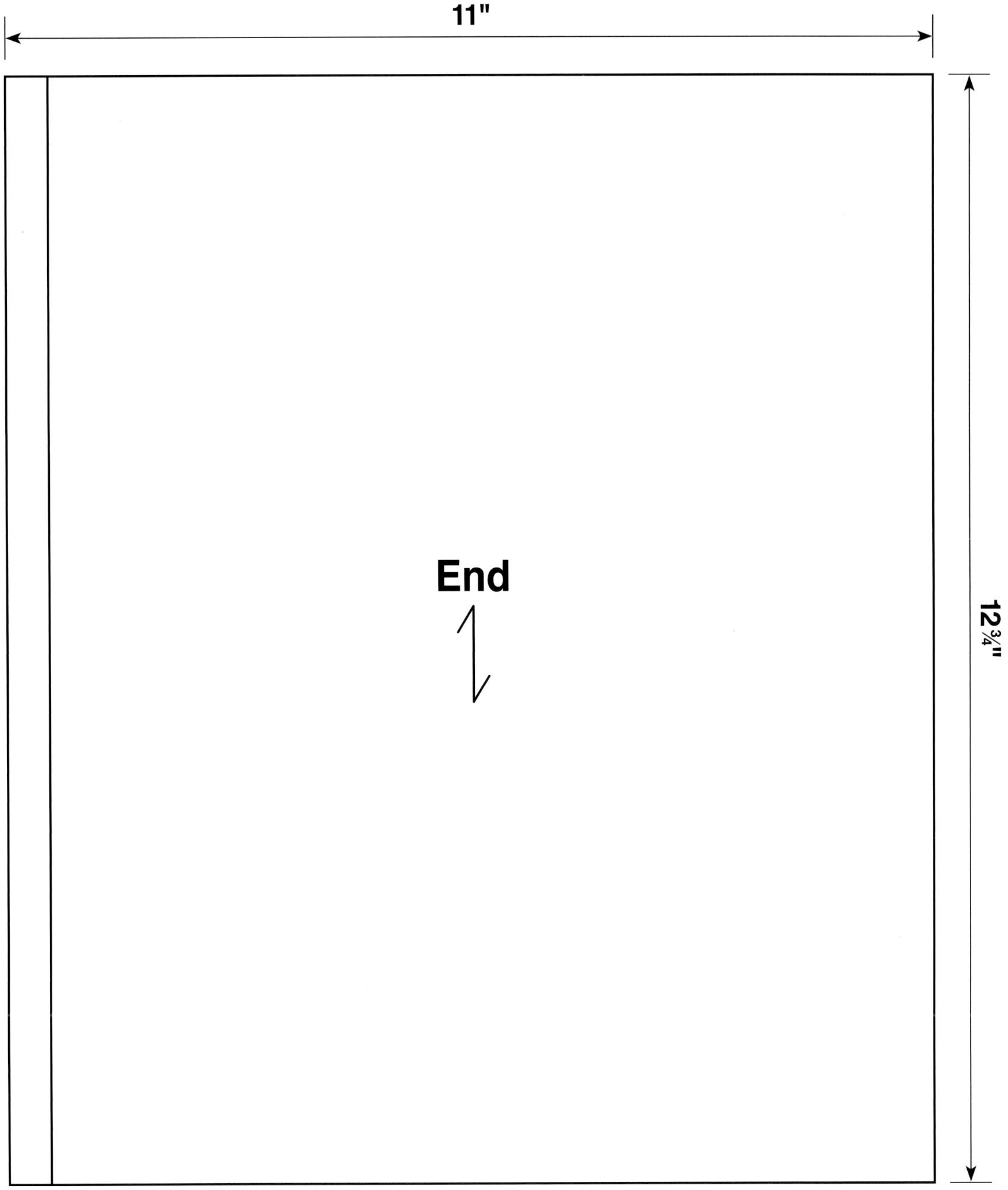

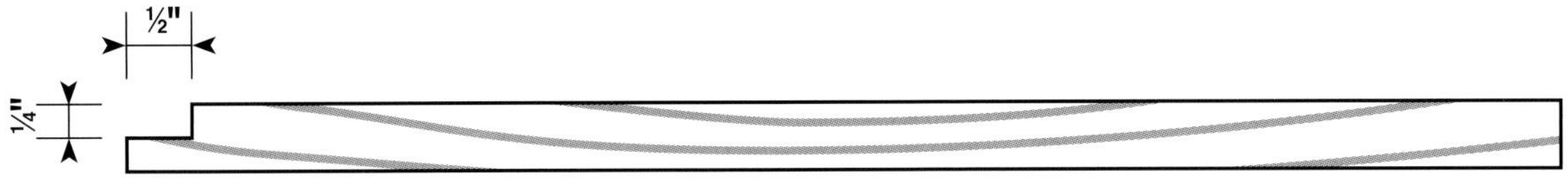

11"

12 ¾"

**End**

½"

¼"

Enlarge 200% to
achieve actual size.

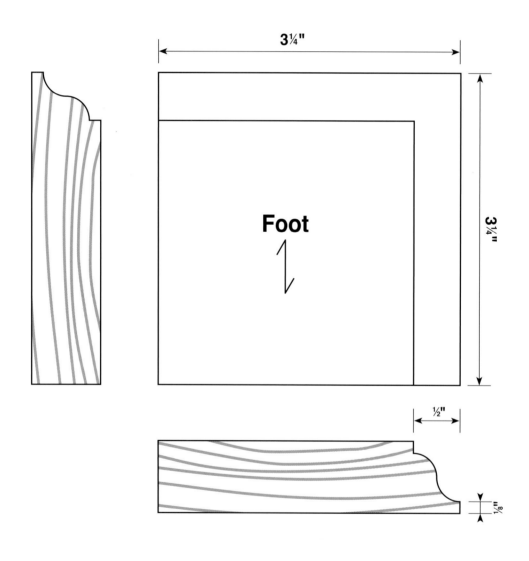

**3¼"**

**3¼"**

**Foot**

**½"**

**⅛"**

Shown actual size.

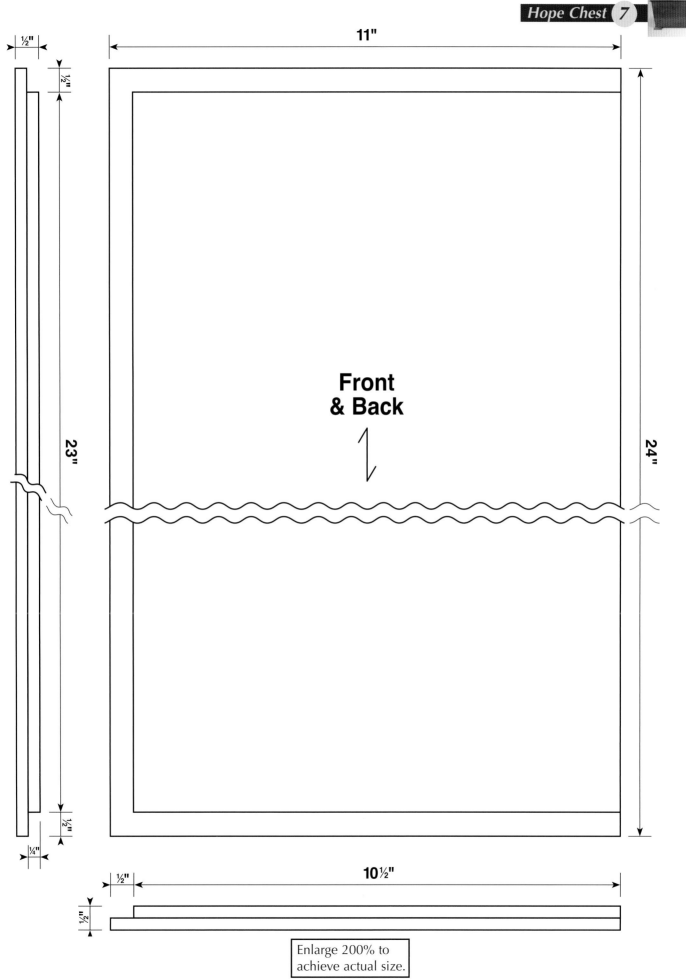

11"

½"

½"

½"

23"

24"

**Front
& Back**

½"

¼"

½"

10½"

½"

Enlarge 200% to
achieve actual size.

**2¼"**

**7"**

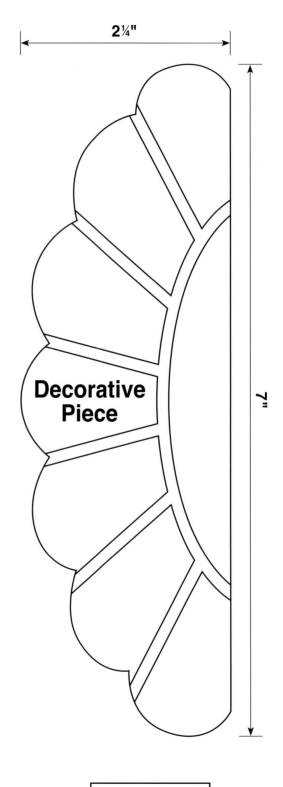

**Decorative
Piece**

Shown actual size.

3"

B B

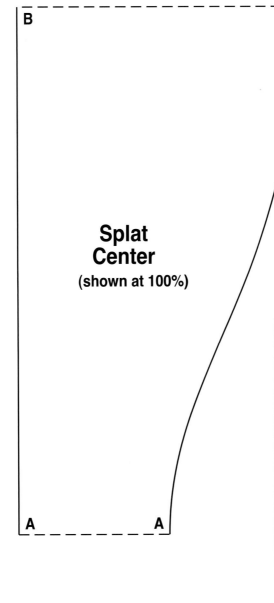

**Splat Center**
(shown at 100%)

A A

24"

A A
A A

B B
B B

**Splat Center**

A A
A A

**Splat End**

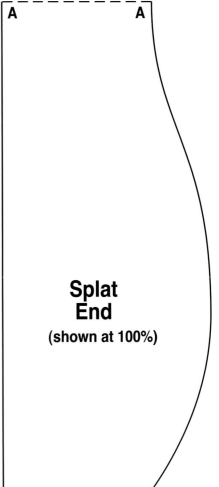

A A

**Splat End**
(shown at 100%)

**NOTE: The composite above is shown at 35% of actual size.**

# *Southwestern-style* *Trunk*

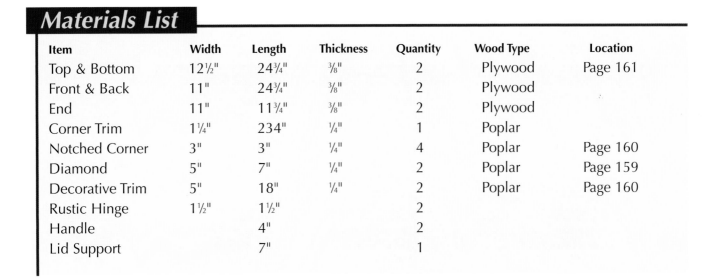

## Materials List

| Item | Width | Length | Thickness | Quantity | Wood Type | Location |
|---|---|---|---|---|---|---|
| Top & Bottom | 12½" | 24¾" | ⅜" | 2 | Plywood | Page 161 |
| Front & Back | 11" | 24¾" | ⅜" | 2 | Plywood | |
| End | 11" | 11¾" | ⅜" | 2 | Plywood | |
| Corner Trim | 1¼" | 234" | ¼" | 1 | Poplar | |
| Notched Corner | 3" | 3" | ¼" | 4 | Poplar | Page 160 |
| Diamond | 5" | 7" | ¼" | 2 | Poplar | Page 159 |
| Decorative Trim | 5" | 18" | ¼" | 2 | Poplar | Page 160 |
| Rustic Hinge | 1½" | 1½" | | 2 | | |
| Handle | | 4" | | 2 | | |
| Lid Support | | 7" | | 1 | | |

# Construction Sequence: Southwestern-Style Trunk

1. Purchase ⅜" AC plywood for this project.
2. Cut the Top & Bottom pieces to the sizes specified on the drawing.
3. Cut a ⅜" x ³⁄₁₆" rabbet on all edges of the Top & Bottom piece as specified on the drawing.
4. Cut the Ends and the Front & Back pieces to the sizes specified on the materials list.
5. Apply glue to each end of the End pieces and clamp them to the Front & Back pieces. Ensure that the assembly is square.
6. Apply glue to the rabbet cut in the Top & Bottom pieces and clamp these to the assembly to create a totally enclosed box.
7. Cut six Corner Trim pieces for the 24¾" length across the Front, the Back and the Top.
8. Apply glue and use ½" brad nails to attach the Corner Trim pieces to the Box Assembly.
9. Cut six Corner Trim pieces for the 12½" Ends. Use glue and nails to attach them to the Box Assembly.
10. Cut eight Corner Trim pieces for the 10½" vertical corners of the Box Assembly. Use glue and nails to attach these to the Box Assembly.
11. Photocopy the pattern for the Notched Corner pieces. Use temporary adhesive to attach the photocopy to the wood selected for these pieces. Cut out the four Notched Corner pieces.
12. Apply glue and use ½" brad finish nails to attach these pieces to the corners of the Top.
13. Photocopy the pattern for the Decorative Trim. Use temporary adhesive to attach the photocopy to the wood selected for these pieces. Cut out the two Diamond pieces using a scroll saw or a band saw.
14. Apply glue and use ½" brad finish nails to attach these Diamond pieces in the center of each End.
15. Photocopy the pattern for the Diamond Trim. Use temporary adhesive to attach the photocopy to the wood selected for these pieces. Cut out the two Diamond Trim pieces using a scroll saw or a band saw.
16. Apply glue and use ½" brad finish nails to attach these Diamond Trim pieces in the center of the Top and the Front.
17. Use a woodcarving gouge to cut random grooves in the Notched Corner, the Diamond Trim and the Decorative Trim pieces. This gives the wood a weathered, rustic look after a stain is applied.
18. Cut the Box Assembly to separate the lid from the remainder of the box. The lid thickness should be 1½". (Cut along the edge of the Notched Corner attached to the Front of the box.) This can be done using a table saw or jigsaw.

19. Cut one more Notched Corner piece 22¼" long. Apply glue and use ½" brad finish nails to attach this piece to the top edge of the Back.
20. Install two Rustic Hinges 3" from the ends to join the box to the lid.
21. Install two rustic drawer pulls to the Ends to use as Handles.
22. Install Lid Support hardware inside the box, if desired.
23. Sand the trunk inside and out and apply a stain and a finish.

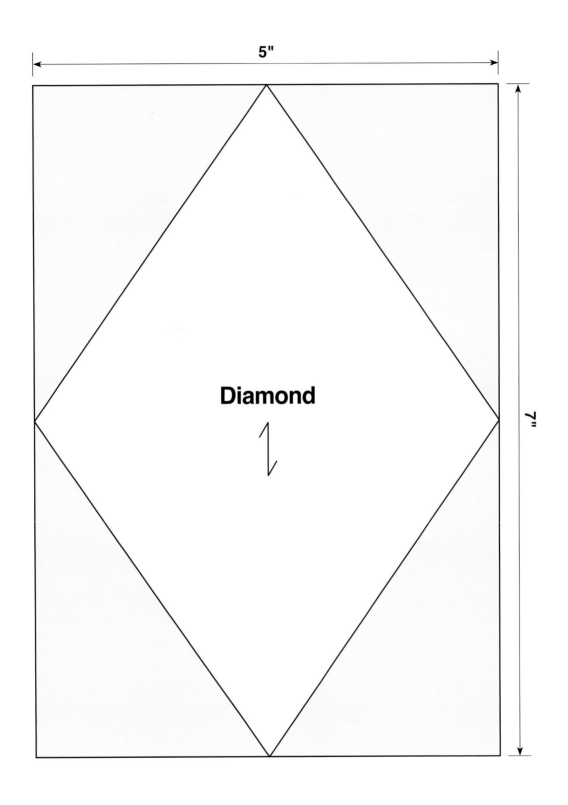

**5"**

**7"**

**Diamond**

Shown actual size.

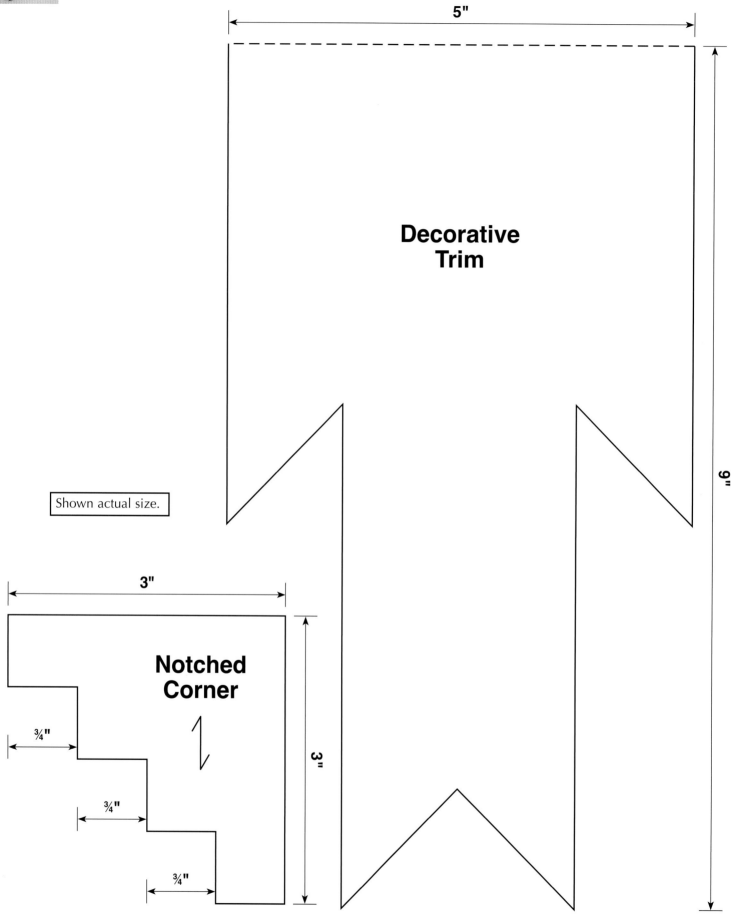

5"

**Decorative Trim**

9"

Shown actual size.

3"

**Notched Corner**

3"

¾"

¾"

¾"

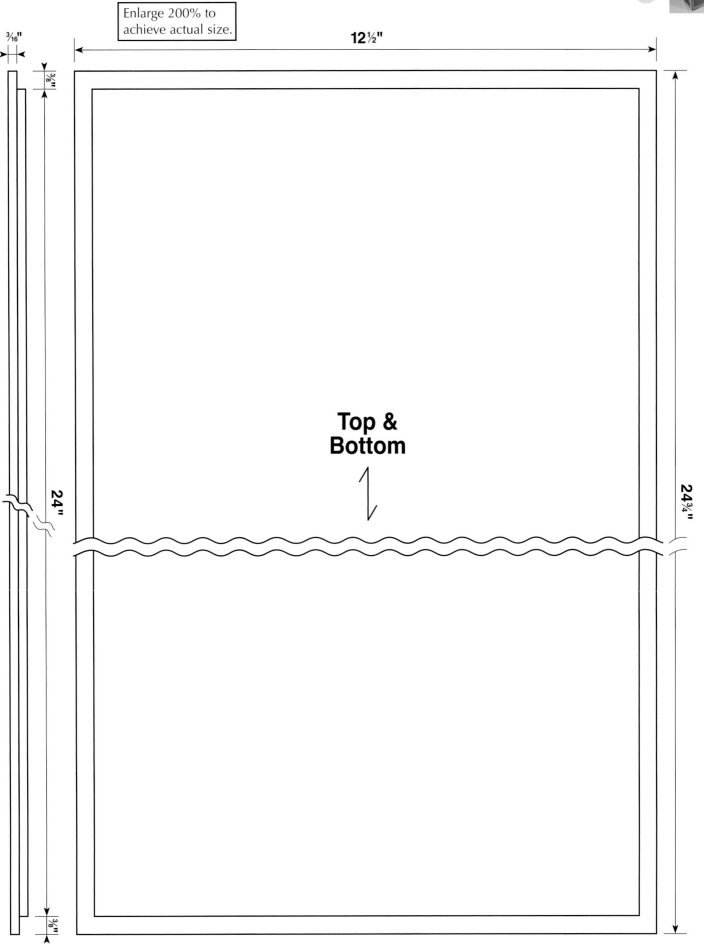

Enlarge 200% to achieve actual size.

3/16"

3/8"

12½"

24"

24¾"

**Top & Bottom**

3/8"

# *Traveling Case*

## Materials List

| Item | Width | Length | Thickness | Quantity | Wood Type | Location |
|------|-------|--------|-----------|----------|-----------|----------|
| Top & Bottom | 10" | 20" | ⅜" | 2 | Plywood | Page 166 |
| Side | 8" | 19¾" | ⅜" | 2 | Plywood | |
| End | 8" | 10" | ⅜" | 2 | Plywood | Page 165 |
| Hanger Rod | | 7" | | 1 | Soft wire | Page 165 |
| Vinyl #1 | 24" | 34" | | 2 | Vinyl Paper | Page 167 |
| Vinyl #2 | 11" | 21" | | 2 | Vinyl Paper | |
| Vinyl #3 | 3¾" | 60" | | 2 | Vinyl Paper | |
| Hanger | | 13" | | 4 | Soft wire | Page 164 |
| Hasp | | 2⅜" | | 2 | Brass | |
| Hinge | | 2½" | | 2 | Brass | |
| Corner | | 1" | | 8 | Brass | |
| Handle | | 4~6" | | 1 | Plastic | |

# Construction Sequence:  Traveling Case

## Making the Traveling Case Assembly

1. Purchase ⅜" AC plywood for this project.
2. Cut all the plywood pieces to the sizes specified on the drawings and the materials list.
3. Cut a ⅜" x 1¼" rabbet on the Top & Bottom pieces as specified on the drawing.
4. Cut a ⅜" x ¼" rabbet on the 8" width for the Ends as specified on the drawing.
5. Dry fit all of the pieces for the box.
6. Apply glue to the rabbet cut in the Ends and clamp the Sides to the Ends. Ensure that the assembly is square.
7. Apply glue to the rabbet cut in the Top & Bottom pieces and clamp the Top & Bottom pieces to the assembly to create a totally enclosed box.
8. Use a router with a pilot-guided ¼" round over bit on all eight edges of the Box Assembly.
9. Cut the assembly in two separate pieces, each being 4" tall.

## Installing the Covering Material

10. Sand the Box Assembly, inside and out. Smooth all the rounded edges and corners.
11. Apply a coat of primer to the Box Assembly, inside and out. Sand the primer after it dries and apply a second coat, if needed.
12. Purchase a single roll of heavy-duty vinyl wallpaper.
13. Coat the Box Assembly inside and out with wallpaper sizing.
14. Cut a section of wallpaper that will cover the Top, the Sides and the Ends and extend 3" on the insides of these surfaces. Reference the measurement specified on the Vinyl #1 drawing.
15. Follow the wallpaper manufacturer's directions to wet and book the wallpaper.
16. Apply the wallpaper to the Box Assembly and smooth out the wrinkles. Because of the rounded corners, the wallpaper will not fit well in the corners. These corners will be covered later by the Corner pieces.

17. Cut a piece of wallpaper to cover the inside of the Top & Bottom pieces. This piece should be oversized to overlap the Sides. Reference the measurements specified on the Vinyl #2 drawing. Apply this piece, following the steps outlined above.

18. Cut a piece of wallpaper to cover the insides of the Sides. This band strip will cover the edges where the previous pieces ended. Reference the measurements specified on the Vinyl #3 drawing. Apply this piece, following the steps outlined above.

## Installing the Hardware

19. Install the metal Corner protectors to all eight corners of the Box Assembly.
20. Install surface-mounted Hinges 3" in from the ends.
21. Install the Hasps on the front of the Box Assembly 3" in from the ends.
22. A Handle could be installed on one end of the Box Assembly, if desired.
23. The Hanger Rod is made using a piece of soft wire. Bend it to the size specified on the drawing. Twist the ends of the wire with needle nose pliers to form a screw loop on each end.
24. Attach the Hanger Rod to the inside of the Box Assembly using ½"-long screws.
25. Wire Hangers may be made by following the drawing. Use a length of wire approximately 13" long for each Hanger.

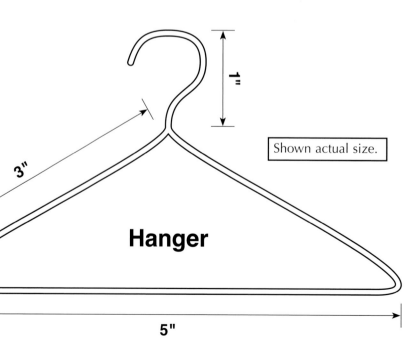

**Hanger**

3"

1"

Shown actual size.

5"

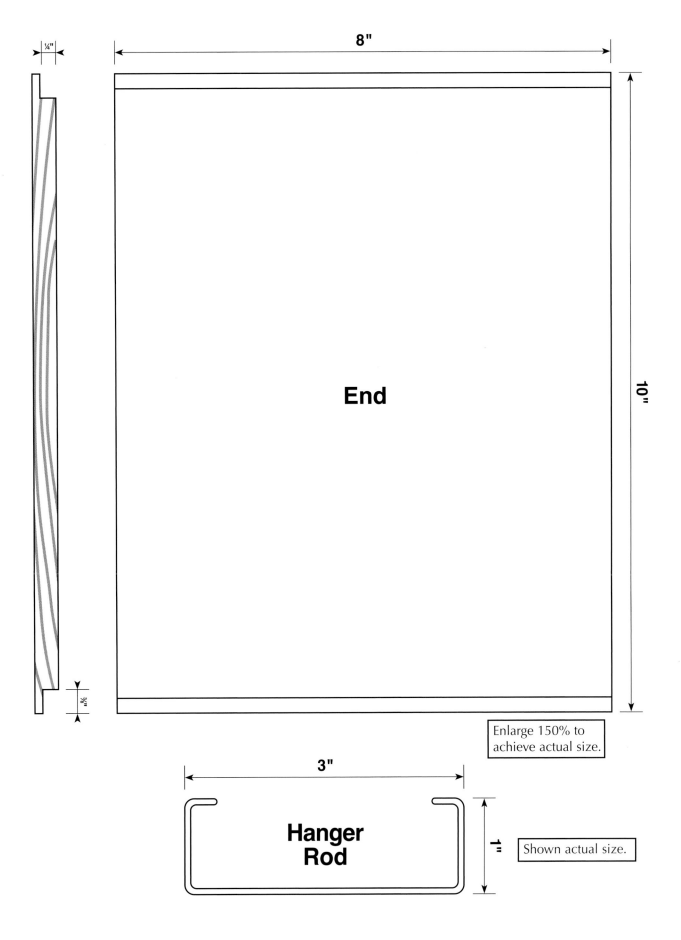

¼"

8"

10"

**End**

⅜"

Enlarge 150% to achieve actual size.

3"

**Hanger Rod**

1"

Shown actual size.

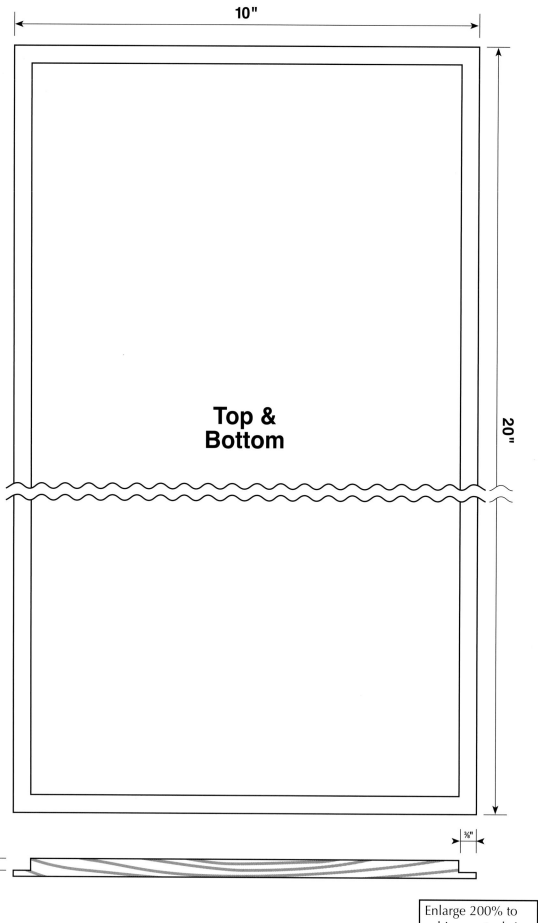

10"

20"

**Top & Bottom**

¼"

⅜"

Enlarge 200% to achieve actual size.

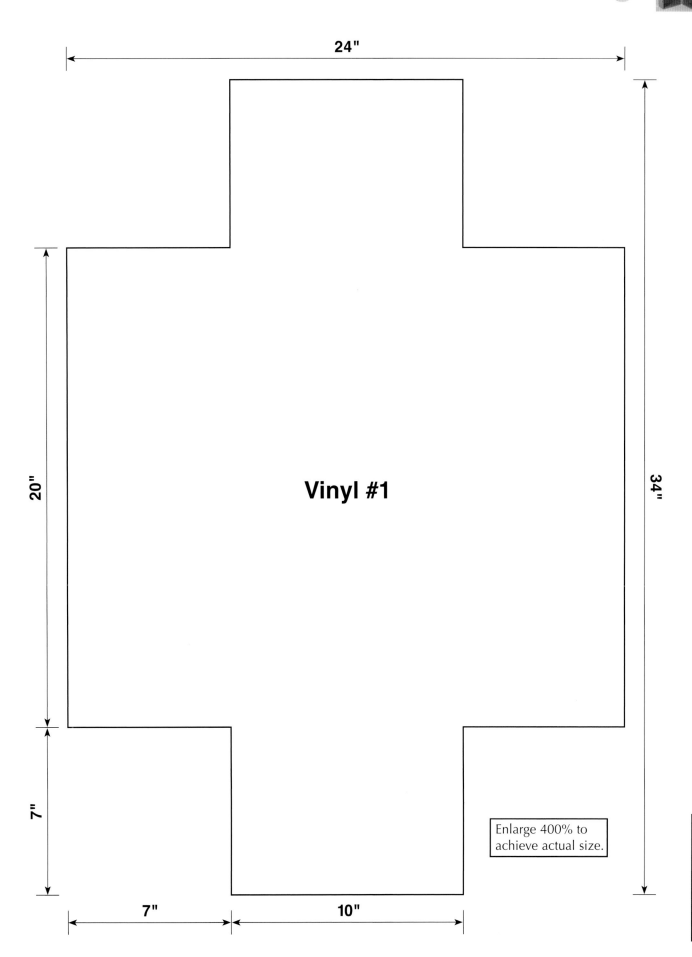

24"

20"

34"

**Vinyl #1**

7"

Enlarge 400% to
achieve actual size.

7"

10"

# *Classic Trunk*

## Materials List

| Item | Width | Length | Thickness | Quantity | Wood Type | Location |
|---|---|---|---|---|---|---|
| Bottom | 13" | 24½" | ⅜" | 1 | Plywood | |
| Front & Back | 9" | 24½" | ⅜" | 2 | Plywood | |
| End | 9" | 12¼" | ⅜" | 2 | Plywood | |
| Edge Trim | 1¼" | 150" | ¼" | 1 | Pine or Poplar | |
| Corner Trim | 2" | 6½" | ¼" | 8 | Pine or Poplar | Page 172 |
| Lid End | 4⅞" | 14¼" | ½" | 2 | Pine or Poplar | Page 173 |
| Lid Rib | 4⅜" | 13¼" | ½" | 2 | Pine or Poplar | Page 176 |
| Lid Front & Back | 2" | 24½" | ½" | 2 | Pine or Poplar | Page 172 |
| Lid Top Slat | 4¼" | 24½" | ½" | 1 | Pine or Poplar | Page 175 |
| Lid Angle Slat | 5¾" | 24½" | ½" | 2 | Pine or Poplar | Page 175 |
| Tray End | 4¼" | 10⅞" | ½" | 2 | Pine or Poplar | Page 174 |
| Tray Side | 3" | 23⅜" | ½" | 2 | Pine or Poplar | Page 174 |
| Tray Bottom | 11⅜" | 22⅞" | ¼" | 1 | Plywood | |
| Tray Support | 1¼" | 12¼" | ¾" | 2 | Pine or Poplar | Page 176 |
| Hinge | 1⅜"‴ | 2" | | 2 | | |
| Hasp | 1" | 2" | | 1 | | |
| Handle | | 4" | | 2 | | |
| Lid Support | | 7" | | 1 | | |

# Construction Sequence: Classic Trunk

## Making the Box Assembly

1. Cut the plywood materials to the sizes specified on the materials list for the Bottom, the Front & Back and the Ends.
2. Cut a ⅜" x ¼" rabbet on all edges of the Bottom as specified.
3. Apply glue to the rabbets in the Bottom piece and to each end of the Ends.
4. Clamp the Ends to the Front & Back and Bottom pieces to make the Box Assembly. Ensure that the assembly is square.
5. Rip cut 150" of ¼"-thick wood to a width of 1¼" for the Edge Trim.
6. Cut four pieces of the Edge Trim materials 24½" long.
7. Apply glue and use ½"-long brad finish nails to attach two of the Edge Trim pieces flush with the top edge on the Front & Back of the Box Assembly.
8. Cut four Edge Trim pieces 13" long for the Ends.
9. Apply glue and use ½"-long brad finish nails to attach two of the Edge Trim pieces to the top edge on the Ends.
10. Photocopy the pattern for the Corner Trim pieces. Use temporary adhesive to attach the photocopy to a scrap piece of ¼" plywood. Cut a wood template for the Corner Trim pieces.
11. Use the wood template to lay out and cut eight Corner Trim pieces.
12. Apply glue and use ½"-long brad finish nails to attach four of the Corner Trim pieces to the Ends. Ensure that these Corner Trim pieces are flush with the Front & Back respectively.

13. Apply glue and use ½"-long brad finish nails to attach the remaining four Corner Trim pieces to the corners on the Front & Back. Ensure that these Corner Trim pieces are flush with the Corner Trim pieces installed in the previous step.

14. Apply glue and use ½"-long brad finish nails to attach the remaining Edge Trim pieces to the bottom edge of the Front & Back and the Ends respectively.

---

**Technical Note:**

The overall size of the Box Assembly should be 25" long x 13½" wide and 9" high. If your results are different, please note this difference. Changes will need to be made to the overall size when making the Lid Assembly.

---

## Making the Lid Assembly

15. Cut the materials for the Lid Ends using ⅜" wood.
16. Cut a ½" x ¼" rabbet on the edges of the Lid Ends as specified on the drawing.
17. Cut two Lid Ribs to the size specified on the drawing.
18. Cut two pieces for the Lid Front & Back pieces.
19. Cut a ½" x ¼" rabbet on one edge of each Lid Front & Back piece as specified on the drawing.
20. Cut one Lid Top Slat and two Lid Angle Slats to the sizes specified on the drawing.
21. Cut 75-degree miters on the edges of the Lid Top and the Angle Slats.
22. Dry assemble the Lid Assembly to ensure a good fit at all connecting points. Confirm that the overall size is 25" long x 13½" wide. Confirm that this size matches the overall size of the Box Assembly measured in the technical note above.
23. Apply glue to the rabbet where the Lid Front attaches to the Lid Ends. Use 1¼"-long brad finish nails to attach the Lid Front & Back pieces to the Lid Ends. Ensure that the rabbet cuts in the Lid Front & Back pieces are oriented up and facing toward the inside of the trunk lid.
24. Measure and mark the location where the Lid Ribs will attach to the Lid Front & Back pieces. The Lid Ribs are located 8" in from each end.
25. Apply glue and attach the Lid Ribs to the Lid Assembly using 1¼"-long brad finish nails. Ensure that the Lid Ribs are square with the Lid Assembly and that the top edge is flush with the rabbets on the Lid Ends.
26. Apply glue to the rabbet areas in the Lid Front piece and Lid End where the Lid Angle Slat will attach. Use 1¼"-long brad finish nails to attach the Lid Angle Slat to the Lid Assembly.
27. Follow this same procedure to attach the other Lid Angle Slat to the Lid Assembly.
28. Check the fit of the Lid Top Slat with the Lid Angle Slats. Adjust the width, if necessary, to accomplish a tight-fitting joint.
29. Apply glue to the mitered edges of the Lid Top Slat and all of the contact areas with the Lid Assembly. Use 1¼"-long brad finish nails to attach this Lid Top Slat to the Lid Assembly.
30. Use a nail set to recess the brad nails below the wood surface. Use wood filler to fill the nail holes.

## Making the Tray Assembly

31. The finished tray size will be 11⅞" x 23⅜". Confirm that this size matches the overall size of the Box Assembly measured in the technical note above.
32. Cut a piece of wood 22" long for the Tray Ends.
33. Cut a piece of wood 47" long for the Tray Sides.
34. Cut a ¼" x 1¼" dado groove in the Tray Ends and in the Tray Sides as specified on the drawings.
35. Cut a piece of ¼" plywood for the Tray Bottom.
36. Cut the Tray Sides to the length specified on the drawing.

37. Cut the Tray Ends to the length specified on the drawing.

38. Photocopy the drawing for the Tray Ends. Use temporary adhesive to attach the photocopy to the wood pieces for the Tray Ends.

39. Drill pilot holes for the Handle holes. Cut the Handle holes and the angle cuts on the Tray Ends.

40. Apply glue to both ends of the Tray Ends and to the dado grooves in all of the pieces. Use 1¼"-long brad finish nails to attach the Tray Front to the Tray Ends.

41. Cut two Tray Support pieces to ¾" x 1¼" x 12¼" long. Attach the Tray Supports inside the trunk Ends, using glue and 1"-long brad finish nails. Align these Tray Supports 2¾"" down from the top edge of the Box Assembly.

## Attaching the Lid to the Trunk Assembly

42. Mark the location for the Hinges 4" in from the Ends. Drill pilot holes for the screws and attach the Hinges using the screws.

43. Mount the Lid Support to the inside of the lid and attach the Handles to the Ends.

44. Install the Hasp or trunk latches available from your local hardware supplier.

45. Sand the trunk and apply a finish.

46. Stencils are available from your local arts and crafts suppliers.

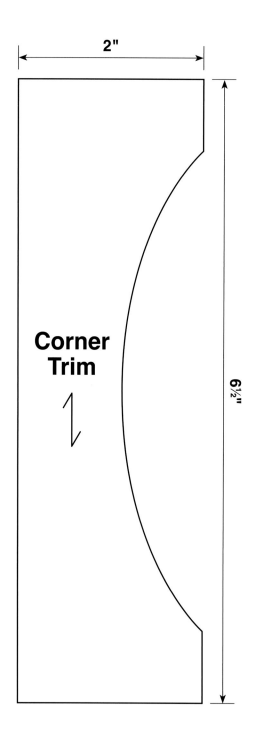

2"

**Corner Trim** ↕

6½"

Shown actual size.

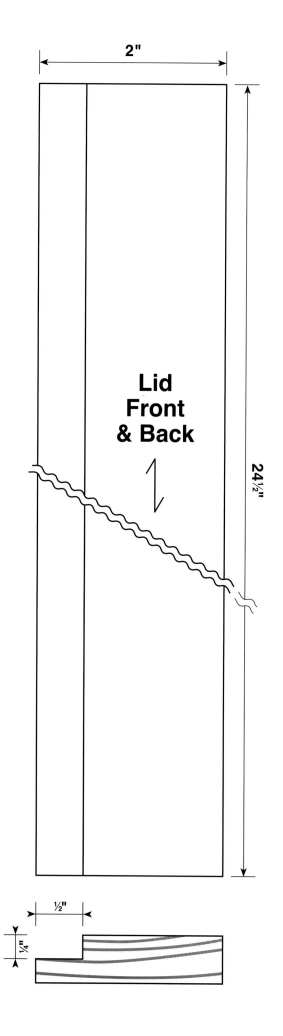

2"

**Lid Front & Back** ↕

24½"

½"

¼"

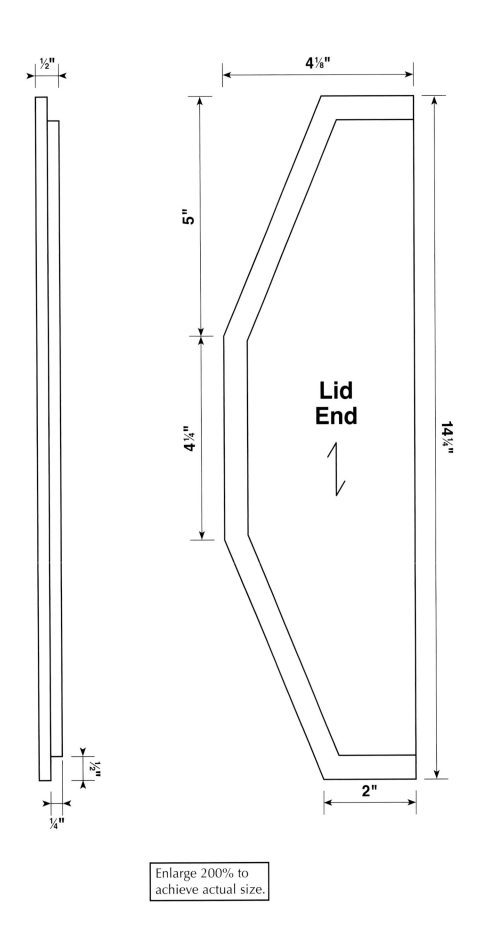

½"

4⅛"

5"

14¼"

4¼"

**Lid End**

½"

¼"

2"

Enlarge 200% to
achieve actual size.

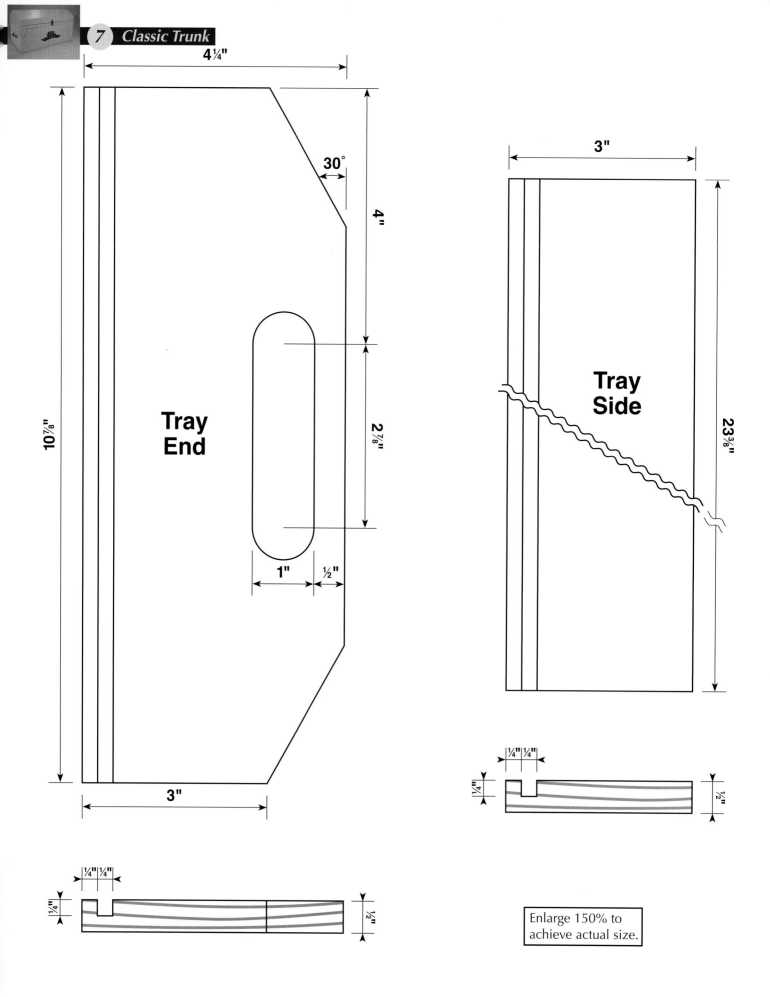

4¼"

30°

4"

Tray
End

2⅞"

10⅞"

1"  ½"

3"

3"

Tray
Side

23⅜"

¼"  ¼"

¼"  ½"

¼"  ¼"

¼"  ½"

Enlarge 150% to
achieve actual size.

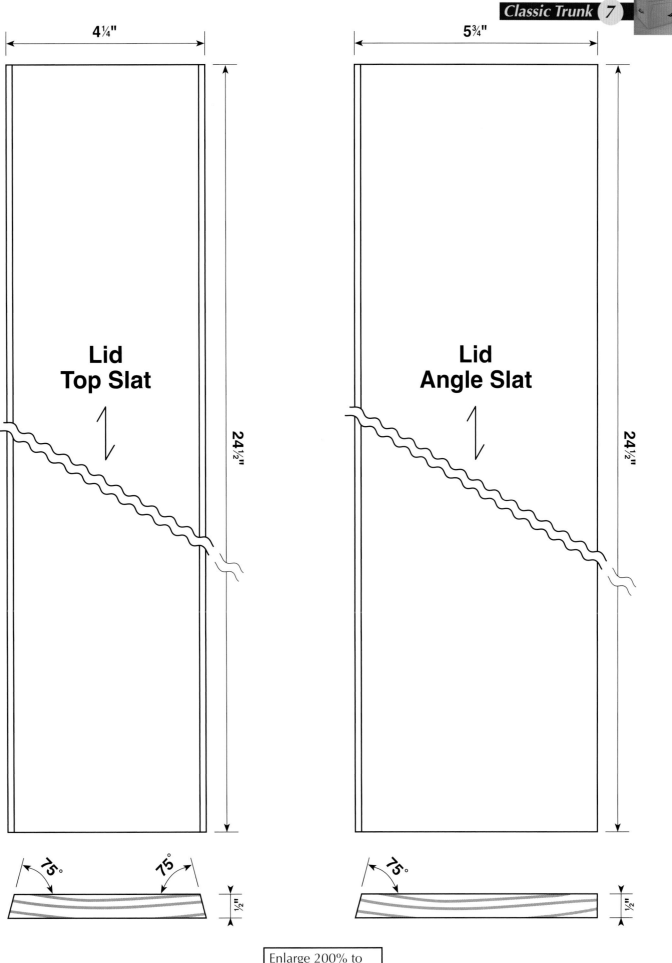

4¼"

**Lid
Top Slat**

24½"

½"

75°    75°

5¾"

**Lid
Angle Slat**

24½"

½"

75°

Enlarge 200% to
achieve actual size.

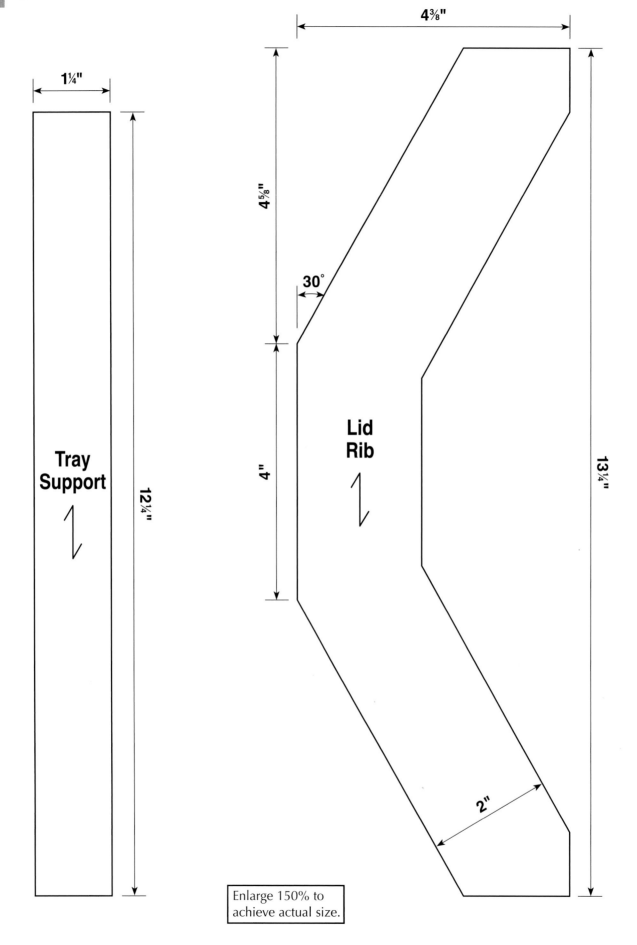

1¼"

4⅜"

4⅝"

30°

4"

**Tray Support**

**Lid Rib**

12¼"

13¼"

2"

Enlarge 150% to achieve actual size.